Hooked Rugs Today

Amy Oxford

Photography by Cynthia McAdoo

Strong Women
Flowers
Animals
Children
Christmas
Miniatures
and More

2006

4880 Lower Valley Road, Atglen, PA 19310 USA

Other Schiffer Books by Amy Oxford
Hooked Rugs Today
Punch Needle Rug Hooking: Techniques and Designs

Other Schiffer Books on Related Subjects
Hooked on Rugs: Outstanding Contemporary Designs, by Jessie A. Turbayne
The Big Book of Hooked Rugs: 1950-1980s, by Jessie A. Turbayne
The Complete Guide to Collecting Hooked Rugs: Unrolling the Secrets, by Jessie A. Turbayne
The Hooker's Art: Evolving Designs in Hooked Rugs, by Jessie A. Turbayne
Contemporary Hooked Rugs: Themes and Memories, by Linda Rae Coughlin

Library of Congress Cataloging-in-Publication Data

Oxford, Amy.
  Hooked rugs today : strong women, flowers, animals, children, christmas, miniatures, and more / Amy Oxford ; photography by Cynthia McAdoo.
      p. cm.
  Includes bibliographical references and index.
  ISBN 0-7643-2578-7 (pbk.)
  1. Rugs, Hooked—United States—History—21st century—Themes, motives. I. Title.

NK2812.O962 2006
746.7'4'0973—dc22   2006021977

Copyright © 2006 by Amy Oxford

Covers and book designed by: Bruce Waters
Type set in Zapf Humanist DmBT/Arrus BT

ISBN: 0-7643-2578-7
Printed in China

The photograph of Patty Yoder's "T is for Toby" rug is courtesy of Ramsey Yoder.

Background information on The Round Barn and Shelburne Museum (page 9), © Shelburne Museum, Shelburne, Vermont.

Rug measurements have been rounded off to the nearest inch while miniature rugs have been rounded to the nearest quarter inch.

The Green Mountain Rug Hooking Guild's rug show is not juried. Any of our members can be a part of the exhibit. Similarly, this book embraces all of our guild members, including experienced rug hookers, beginners, and children.

Every possible attempt to properly identify and acknowledge the names of rug designers and pattern companies has been made by both the rug hookers and the author. If needed, corrections can be made to future editions as long as the author is notified.

Front cover images (clockwise, from top right): Melissa's Fairy. Designed and hooked by Kathleen Menzies; Twelve Drummers Drumming. Designed and hooked by Susanne McNally; Khotan. Hooked by Darcy Cardas, designed by Jane McGown Flynn; My Turkish Lady. Designed and hooked by Betty Oberstar; Friendship. Hooked by Carol T. Dale and designed by Gardner King; Katie. Designed and hooked by Patricia Merikallio.

Back cover images (left to right): Three French Hens. Designed and hooked by Donna Hrkman; Boris. Designed and hooked by Patricia Merikallio; Prince Sasha. Designed and hooked by Janet Wagner; Indigo Bunting. Designed and hooked by Ian A. Hodgdon

Published by Schiffer Publishing Ltd.
4880 Lower Valley Road
Atglen, PA 19310
Phone: (610) 593-1777; Fax: (610) 593-2002
E-mail: Info@schifferbooks.com

For the largest selection of fine reference books on this and related subjects, please visit our web site at **www.schifferbooks.com**
We are always looking for people to write books on new and related subjects. If you have an idea for a book please contact us at the above address.

This book may be purchased from the publisher.
Include $3.95 for shipping.
Please try your bookstore first.
You may write for a free catalog.

In Europe, Schiffer books are distributed by
Bushwood Books
6 Marksbury Ave.
Kew Gardens
Surrey TW9 4JF England
Phone: 44 (0) 20 8392-8585; Fax: 44 (0) 20 8392-9876
E-mail: info@bushwoodbooks.co.uk
Website: www.bushwoodbooks.co.uk
Free postage in the U.K., Europe; air mail at cost.

Contents

The companion volume to this book features Green Mountain Rug Hooking Guild Honorees Michele Micarelli and Emily K. Robertson. Also included are rugs in the following categories: people, geometrics, fruits, flower baskets, cabbage roses, landscapes, holidays, accessories, and more animals (dogs, horses, donkeys, chickens, roosters, insects, monkeys, reptiles, fish, rabbits, and many other wonderful beasts).

Dedication

Dedicated to the memory of our friend, Patty Yoder, 1943-2005.
Green Mountain Rug Hooking Guild President
October, 2001 – March, 2005.

When our last book was released, Patty was the first to see it, hot off the press. She was so happy and excited about the book that she hugged it to herself protectively and smiled, saying, "No one is allowed to say anything bad in front of this book. Ever. Not one mean word." She cared deeply about the guild, about us, and our art. So remember, be careful what you say in front of this book.

T is for Toby. Designed and hooked by Patty Yoder. 50" by 31". This rug, taken from Patty's book *The Alphabet of Sheep*, depicts Patty with two members of her beloved flock.

Acknowledgments

I would like to sincerely thank you, the members of The Green Mountain Rug Hooking Guild, for your enthusiasm and for your support of this book. Most of all, I would like to thank you for making all these incredible rugs. It has been a pleasure to be surrounded by your artwork during these months of book building. Your photographs are truly inspiring, but your quotes also have the encouraging effect of making me want to try new techniques, learn more, take classes, hoard wool, get out my dye pots, and start a new rug. Your love of the craft is contagious and will inspire many others to pick up a hook.

Sincere thanks to Cynthia McAdoo for photographing all the rugs. Being an art photographer sounds glamorous, but a four day outdoor photo shoot in twenty degree weather with snow tends to take away some of the romance. Cynthia was always a good sport, an intrepid photographer in five layers of clothing. Anything to get good lighting. She made the shoot run like clockwork. Besides taking the pictures, she spent months in her digital darkroom getting the best possible color and quality, manually removing the backdrop behind every rug, looking for things that only a trained eye could see. If I had a loop for every time I asked her advice on this project, I could have made a hall runner by now. Thank goodness she is so funny. That has been the happiest part about making this book.

Many thanks to rug show co-chairs Rae Harrell and Barbara Held. Your vision for the show, your skill and fortitude, and your ability to not faint when faced with an unexpected and staggering 940 rugs is truly remarkable. Rising to the occasion, you somehow doubled our wall space without making the show feel crowded. Hats off to you for a remarkable job.

I am thankful for the help of my editors, Tina Skinner and Donna Baker, for their assistance and expertise, and for giving me the freedom to make the kind of book I had in mind.

Many thanks to Shelburne Museum for hosting our rug show for the past six years and special thanks to Museum Director Stephan Jost for his interest in our craft and his support of our exhibition. Thanks must also be given to the Museum's Visitor Services Manager, Bruce Andrews, who makes the whole idea of transforming a barn into an art show seem not only possible, but festive. Thanks to Monty Stokes for all his work behind the scenes, setting the stage for the exhibit.

I am eternally grateful to the following guild members who worked with care, professionalism, and good cheer to help photograph the rugs: Nancy Baker, Angelika Brumbaugh, Carolyn Buttolph, Janet Conner, Cheryl Connor, Jerry Connor, Judith Dallegret, Eugenie Delaney, Judith English, Liam English, Fiona Fenwick, Pandy Goodbody, Jane Griswold, Jocelyn Guindon, Joan Hebert, Priscilla Heininger, Layne Herschel, Stephanie Krauss, Gail Lapierre, Rachelle LeBlanc, Kevin McLoughlin, Ruth McLoughlin, Celia Oliver, Linda Pitkin, Karen Tompson, and Lin Watson. Working in the numbing cold, you kept your eye on every rug, watching out for them as if they were your own.

The unsung heroes of the rug show are a group of women who quietly took home almost one thousand rug registration forms and typed up all the information about each piece. Name, address, rug title, designer, dimensions, and the source of the design in fifty words or less. No small task. Especially since there were often fifty words or more. These women then turned all this information into beautiful labels for the show. Many thanks to Nancy Bachand, Nancy Baker, Gail Lapierre, Bonnie LaPine, Jane Ploof and Maureen Yates. When they were done, Maureen Yates expertly e-mailed all this information to me, making this book possible. Her help was invaluable.

Heartfelt thanks to Anne-Marie Littenberg for all her hard work on this project. Not only was she always ready to lend an ear, she wrote the foreword, the vendor list, and the most thorough rug hooking bibliography I've ever seen. She offered many helpful suggestions and was also a proofreader.

I would like to express sincere gratitude to my mother, Julie Righter, for proofreading; to Judy English for making dozens of phone calls to track down missing information; to Shirley Zandy and Maureen Yates for helping with the index; to all of the rug designers and rug shop owners who assisted me when I was trying to give credit where credit was due; and to Andréa

Borriello, Lindsay Boyer, Mark Boyer, Linda Rae Coughlin, Alaina Dickason, Susan Feller, Lee Greenewalt, Ben Harper, Preston McAdoo, Barb Moyer, Lynette Noble, Celia Oliver, Iris Oxford, Mat Oxford, Don Riley, Suzanne Sawyer, John Soutter, Lucy Soutter, and Ramsey Yoder.

This rug show is made possible by the many guild members who generously volunteer their time. Wholehearted thanks to Jill Aiken, Polly Alexander, Sandy Alsum, Nancy Bachand, Nancy Baker, Donna Beaudoin, Jennie Behr, Nancy Birdsall, Kathy Boozan, Betty Bouchard, Angelika Brumbaugh, Diane Burgess, Sara Burghoff, Karen Bushey, Carolyn Buttolph, Shirley Chaiken, Willy Cochran, Janet Conner, Cheryl Connor, Sheila Coogan, Karen Cooper, Judith Dallegret, Eugenie Delaney, Suzanne Dirmaier, Judy Dodds, Lory Doolittle, Betty Edwards, Judith English, Fiona Fenwick, Maddy Fraioli, Diana Gauthier, Stephanie Gibson, Susan Gingras, Pandy Goodbody, Jane Griswold, Jocelyn Guindon, Rae Harrell, Katie Hartner, Joan Hebert, Priscilla Heininger, Barbara Held, Layne Herschel, Mary Hulette, Kathy Hutchins, Rachel Jacobs, Laurie Kass, Debra Kaiser, Diane Kelly, Stephanie Krauss, Cyndi LaBelle, Gail Lapierre, Bonnie LaPine, Jean LaPlant, Jen Lavoie, Rachelle LeBlanc, Diana Link, Sue Longchamps, Sherry Lowe, Anne-Marie Littenberg, Susan Mackey, Delbert Martin, Karen Martin, Raina Mason, Beth McDermett, Kris McDermett, Barbara McKenna, Ruth McLoughlin, Joan Mohrmann, Carol Munson, Lynn Ocone, Mary Lee O'Connor, Fran Oken, Celia Oliver, Bonnie Olson, Trinka Parker, Jane Perry, Carol Petillo, Nancy Phillips, Linda Pitkin, Jane Ploof, Bobbi Pond, Karen Quigley, Dot Rankin, Julie Rogers, Mary Sargent, Arlene Scanlon, Jule Marie Smith, Amy Spokes, Ruth St. George, Karen Tompson, Lin Watson, Johanna White, Helen Wolfel, Maureen Yates, Shirley Zandy, and the many other volunteers who jumped in to help when needed.

Most of all, thank you to Peter.

Can you find this elephant? He is hidden somewhere in this book in one of the rugs. Hint: He is not alone.

6

Foreword

Our guild was founded in 1981 when several dozen Vermont ladies got together, strung a clothesline between some trees on a town green, and hung their rugs to show each other their work. By the time of our most recent gathering in April 2006, our membership had grown to nearly 900 and we had installed an exhibit featuring 940 pieces created by members from as far away as Japan. Our venue has evolved from that old clothesline to the Round Barn at the world-renowned Shelburne Museum, in Shelburne, Vermont. During our quarter of a century, we have become a 501c3 non-profit, dedicated to education about the art and craft of rug hooking. Our membership roster includes the names of some of the world's best known and beloved rug hooking artists, teachers, and writers. How did tiny, rural Vermont become a sort of Mecca for rug hooking?

The answer, of course, is the people—the dedicated rug hookers who love our community of fiber, and the art and craft of rug hooking. Our guild's members are a hardworking, generous bunch. How else could we host such a huge exhibit staffed entirely by volunteers? Our volunteers do everything from managing mailing lists to fabricating walls for installing rugs. And we do it in the extreme cold of Vermont winter. Our first frost of the year can be expected around Labor Day, and our last, around Memorial Day. There are many months of the year when it's cold outside, so we are inside—hooking away.

According to the U.S. Census Bureau, our population is also the most rural in the country. Besides braving the cold, we can be a lonely, isolated group. (More than fifty per cent of Vermont's roads are unpaved!) Our rug hooking brings us together. All over the state, there are numerous formal and informal hooking groups that meet weekly. While we gather to hook and to put together an annual exhibit that is downright sumptuous, we also gather to teach the world about rug hooking. Our education program sends our members into schools, non-profit organizations, and community groups to voluntarily teach rug hooking. The Green Mountain Rug Hooking Guild donates the materials and tools, while our members volunteer to provide the know-how.

Theories about weather and rural living don't, however, explain why our membership comes from all over the world. Our dedicated Vermont members are only a small part of the picture, as we have extraordinary, far-flung members who drive and fly hundreds (even thousands) of miles to be part of our activities. Perhaps one reason we are so fortunate in this regard is the support and nurturing provided to everyone, from the experienced, renowned fiber artist to the neophyte just learning to hook. We honor and treasure the work of all our members, and celebrate it through our annual, non-juried exhibition.

Our rugs are great, but the members of our guild are fabulous!

—Anne-Marie Littenberg
President, Green Mountain Rug Hooking
Guild

Introduction: Welcome to the Rug Show

Hooked in the Mountains XI
The Round Barn, Shelburne Museum,
Shelburne, Vermont
April 1-9, 2006

One rug show visitor, new to the art of rug hooking, summed it all up after looking around for a few minutes and remarking, "I never knew hooked rugs could look like THIS!" To be honest, I don't think our guild members knew either, until they got hooking. Now that they're hitting their stride, they're unstoppable, taking on artistic challenges with daring, surprising themselves and each other.

The rug hookers whose work is shown here range in age from eight to ninety-four. They're able to make rugs that are replicas of hooked pieces from the 1800s, dyeing the wool colors that are correct for the period. At the same time, they can tackle a contemporary piece, simultaneously combining careful technique with creative, reckless abandon. They bring a fresh eye to traditional designs, and are fearless when it comes to stepping out on their own. They are prolific, and the results are exciting.

Based on previous years, we were expecting around 600 rugs for this year's show. We were astonished to get 940. To say we were surprised would be true, but "in shock" would be more accurate. Everyone involved with hanging the show wondered if we would have enough room for the rugs. Where would we put them all? Would they fit? What would we do if they didn't? With Yankee ingenuity and a lot of hard work, these problems were solved. New plywood walls were built. The silo in the center of the round barn, which has always been a great place to show off rugs, was put to maximum use. To ensure that every rug could come to the party, pieces were hung as high on the silo as we could reach this year. Some people were disappointed that all the work wasn't at eye level. Though it was sad not being able to see every small detail on these raised rugs, many visitors loved being able to admire them from a distance, giving them a perspective that few of the lower rugs had. In the end, thanks to many volunteers, all entries were on display, not one on the floor (an odd goal for a rug show). The results were breathtaking. At the opening, I confided to a friend that the exhibit was so delightfully overwhelming that I was unable to talk, eat hors d'oeuvres, and look at the rugs, all at the same time. What a great problem to have!

Of the 940 rugs, 30 are not included here, either for copyright reasons or at the artist's request. The remaining 910 rugs are divided between this book and its companion volume. Imagine having enough rugs to fill two books! It would be interesting to figure out the total square footage of all of these hooked pieces. It could be a contest, like guessing how many jelly beans are in the jar. How many acres of rugs were there at the rug show? Would they cover a football field?

Part of a rug's beauty is its texture and the richness of the fibers. When you see a textile that catches your eye, your natural instinct is to touch it and see what it feels like. This book is the next best thing to experiencing the rug show in person. In addition to the beautiful photographs, the artists' quotes, though brief, provide great insight into the guild members, both individually and as a whole. After reading this book, it will be clear what a thoughtful, creative, sincere, and genuine group this is. They candidly share their hearts, souls, and dreams, telling us where and how to look for them in their artwork. Reading their stories is kind of like sitting around the kitchen table with old friends. They're honest, share their secrets, are delightful to be with, and are often very funny. I hope you enjoy this visit to their rug show.

—Amy Oxford

Shelburne Museum, founded in 1947, is one of the nation's most eclectic museums of art, Americana, architecture, and artifacts. Thirty-nine galleries and exhibition structures display over 150,000 objects spanning four centuries. Outstanding collections of folk art, decorative arts, tools, toys, textiles, and transportation vehicles are exhibited in tandem with paintings by artists such as Monet, Manet, Cassatt, Degas, Andrew Wyeth, Thomas Cole, Winslow Homer, Grandma Moses, and many others. The museum's twenty-five 19th century structures include a covered bridge, a lighthouse, a 220 foot restored steamboat that is a National Historic Landmark, as well as the round barn that houses our rug show and other special events.

Shelburne Museum's round barn was built in 1901 by Fred "Silo" Quimby in East Passumpsic, Vermont. It was moved piece by piece to Shelburne in 1985-1986. The center of the building, a 9000 lb. round silo, could not be taken apart for structural reasons. It was airlifted across the state by a skycrane helicopter and lowered safely onto its new foundation. The three story barn is 80' in diameter and 60' tall and had ties for sixty cows on the middle floor. It was a model of agricultural efficiency, allowing gravity to work to the farmer's advantage. Hay stored on the top level could be lowered down for easy feeding, while manure could drop through trap doors to the basement, directly into the farmer's waiting manure spreader, which was pulled by a team of horses. Less than twenty-four round barns were built in Vermont and many of these have either collapsed or been destroyed by fire. The Shakers built the first round barn in America in 1824 in Hancock, Massachusetts. Photograph © Shelburne Museum, Shelburne, Vermont.

At the center of the round barn is a silo, also round. In this photograph, you can see rugs hanging on the silo (right) and also on one of the many plywood "walls" (left) put up each year especially for the show. According to show co-chair Rae Harrell, "Six years ago we started out with twenty-eight walls (each one made out of a whole sheet of plywood) and gradually added more each year. This year there were so many rugs we had to get thirty more sheets. We now have ninety-eight walls. And that doesn't count all the regular walls of the actual barn." Added Rae, laughing, "That's it, that's as big as we can get! We have an arsenal of walls. Wherever we go, we've got walls!" In addition, after frugally adding a few each year, the guild now owns enough track lighting to illuminate a small town. Photograph © Shelburne Museum, Shelburne, Vermont.

A group of Green Mountain Rug Hooking Guild members at the opening reception of the rug show, Friday, March 31, 2006. The beautiful backdrop, an enlarged version of "Paris Street" designed and hooked by Gwenn C. Smith (see Chapter 9), was later added by photographer Cynthia McAdoo. If you know you posed for this shot but can't find yourself, don't worry, you aren't losing your marbles. Unfortunately, the poor lighting left everyone in the back rows—and some people on the sides—in complete darkness and unrecognizable. Instead of losing the whole picture, Cynthia decided to edit the photograph. We unravel hooking when we don't have enough contrast to see our design, and, though she hated to, Cynthia had to pull out loops of her own. A poor analogy; all of you are more precious than any loops and we are disappointed not to be able to include everyone in this picture.

Chapter 1

Viewers' Choice Awards 2006

When visitors arrive at the rug show, they are given a paper ballot and asked to vote for their favorite rug. This seems like an easy and jolly task until many rugs start competing for your affection. Some years, one rug will steal your heart and be your obvious pick, while other years, torn with indecision, it only seems fair to draw straws. After all the votes are counted, the top ten become our Viewers' Choice Award Winners.

This year's winners are listed here in alphabetical order. Please note that there were actually eleven winners, due to a tie. All rugs were designed by the respective winners, except *Wash Day*, which was designed by Nancy Urbanak of Beaver Brook Crafts. Congratulations to this year's talented recipients.

Sally D'Albora – *Vinnie's Garden*
Sandy Ducharme – *Sunlit Autumn Moose*
Jennifer Woolley Fernandez – *Moonlight Memories*
Jacqueline Hansen – *Maine Coast Scenic*
Rae Harrell – *The Tambourine*
Gail Lapierre – *Don't Let the Sheep Out*
Jen Lavoie – *A Walk (Triptych)*
Anne-Marie Littenberg – *Ask Me Anything*
Gail Smith – *Wash Day*
Jule Marie Smith – *The Great Ruthie Pickle Game Rug*
Marty Dale Wagemaker – *On Sacred Grounds*

Vinnie's Garden. Hooked by Sally D'Albora, Rockville, Maryland. 37" by 40". Design adapted by Sally D'Albora from a painting by Vincent Van Gogh.
"An adaptation of Van Gogh's painting, *Iris*, as a result of a suggestion by a friend to do a flower pattern in a class with Helen Connelly."

Sunlit Autumn Moose. Designed and hooked by Sandy Ducharme, Marshfield, Vermont. 27" by 32".
"Nature is my inspiration. Mother Nature is the 'strongest woman' of all. We are surrounded by her beauty. Getting depth and distance was the biggest challenge. Creating the illusion of fall brambles was one of my favorite parts. I enjoyed creating this rug from start to finish, including designing, dyeing, and hooking."

Moonlight Memories. Designed and hooked by Jennifer Woolley Fernandez, Richmond, Vermont. 24" by 28".
"I have wonderful memories of my mother hooking rugs, and for thirty years I've thought of trying it. This past summer, my niece, Anita, invited me to Chebeague Island, Maine to study with her teacher, Janet Conners. What a wonderful week and of course, I was hooked! This is my first rug."

Maine Coast Scenic. Designed and hooked by Jacqueline Hansen of The 1840 House, Scarborough, Maine. 25" by 31".
"Living on the coast of Maine, I wanted to express the hearty style of the lighthouse keepers, fishermen, and strong women who lived off the coast of Maine in the past. They weathered many storms, and all kinds of weather."

The Tambourine. Designed and hooked by Rae Harrell, Hinesburg, Vermont. 73" by 40".
"This is the fourth in my series, 'An Orchestra of Women.' "

Don't Let the Sheep Out! Designed and hooked by Gail Duclos Lapierre, Shelburne, Vermont. 43" by 55".
"This tessellation of sheep is dedicated to all those lovely sheep who give their wool so that we may hook. I was inspired to make this rug by my son, Andy, who remarked after viewing my wool stash, 'It's a good thing sheep don't have to die for you to have wool, or you'd be responsible for a lot of deaths!' "

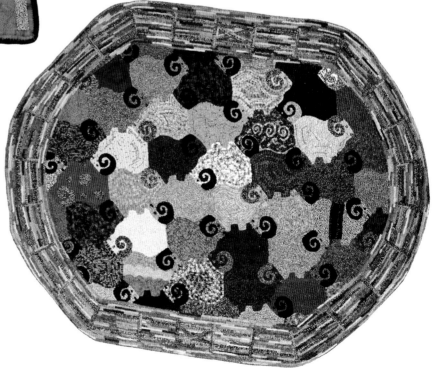

A Walk (Triptych). Designed and hooked by Jen Lavoie, Huntington, Vermont. 36" by 46" each. "This triptych is dedicated to my parents."

Ask Me Anything. Designed and hooked by Anne-Marie Littenberg, Burlington, Vermont. 19" by 28". "An intimate moment in a vast landscape. Is this a scene from a century ago? Is this an ancient Roman road in Italy? For me, it is like a moment in a dream."

Wash Day. Hooked by Gail M. Smith, Weybridge, Vermont. 25" by 32". Designed by Nancy Urbanak of Beaver Brook Crafts.
"When I was a child and clothes were hanging on the line on cold days, my Mom knew how much I hated to do dishes. She would always say to me, 'Gail, I will do the dishes if you go get the clothes off the line.' And of course I would run right out and get them. My mom passed away the year I was hooking this rug. I will always hang this rug over my washing machine and have fond memories of Mom."

The Great Ruthie Pickle Game Rug. Designed and hooked by Jule Marie Smith, Ballston Spa, New York. 36" by 92".
"My kids thought Ruthie needed to grow up imagining life on a rug of her own. The pickle vine is a game board and the first to reach the pickle jar is the winner. Cards matching the dots indicate 'two year old' tasks. This is an Easter present!"

On Sacred Grounds – Part II of My World Trade Center Triptych. Designed and hooked by Marty Dale Wagemaker, Palmyra, New York. 92" by 39".
"For 25 years, New York City was my home. The World Trade Center was one of my favorite places to take my visiting guests. We have to keep the memory alive! I am doing this by hooking a triptych of this area in Lower Manhattan, then, now, and what will be."

On Sacred Grounds

*Silver and gold towers
born free,
do not have to bow,
or get down
on bended knee,*

*Onward and upward,
the heavens call –
an eternal
home for all.*

*This is where our home
will always be, soaring
high and free.*

*On sacred grounds
for eternity.*

©Marty Dale Wagemaker
November 8, 2005

Chapter 2

Viewers' Choice Awards 2005

One of the honors bestowed on the Viewers' Choice Award Winners is having their rugs invited back to the following year's show for visitors to enjoy one more time. The 2005 winners, each making an encore appearance at this year's show, are listed here in alphabetical order. All rugs were designed by the respective winners, except *Buckingham*, which was designed by Jane McGown Flynn. Congratulations to all of these inspirational artists.

Shirley Chaiken – *Kimonos* (not shown)
Sandy Ducharme – *Nature's Harmony*
Ann Hallett – *Who Let the Cows Out?*
Ann Hallett – *The Sheepish Grin – Pin the Tail on the Lamb*
Rae Harrell – *The Flute*
Jen Lavoie – *Woman in Red Wool Suit*
Anne-Marie Littenberg – *Let's Play in the Moonlight*
Joan Mohrmann – *Buckingham*
Lori Lupe Pelish – *Seriously Swirled* (not shown)
Suzi Prather – *Wanna Play* (not shown)

Who Let the Cows Out? Designed and hooked by Ann Hallett, Coldwater, Ontario, Lokieo, Canada. 39" by 50".
"Genetics has been a fascination of mine since childhood. Our gray tabby cat had a litter of colored kittens—one orange, one black, one striped, one black and white. Wow! Holstein cows have markings as unique as our fingerprints. It was fun writing messages on the cows."

Nature's Harmony. Designed and hooked by Sandy Ducharme, Marshfield, Vermont. 50" by 40".
"Nature is my inspiration. Looking out my window at the birds and critters inspired me to capture that feeling in a rug. This is my first original piece and only my second hooking project. I enjoyed designing, dyeing, and hooking it. My sisters-in-law were my inspiration to try rug hooking, and I'm hooked!"

The Sheepish Grin – Pin the Tail on the Lamb.
Designed and hooked by Ann Hallett, Coldwater,
Ontario, Lokieo, Canada. 58" by 34".
"While I was cleaning out the freezer, a mysterious Ziploc® bag surfaced. It contained fourteen lambs' tails. Talk about inspiration! The local taxidermist was my next stop and a rug was born. Pin the tail on the lamb."

The Flute. Designed and hooked by Rae Harrell, Hinesburg, Vermont. 80" by 40".

Woman in Red Wool Suit. Designed and hooked by Jen Lavoie, Huntington, Vermont. 36" by 60".

Let's Play in the Moonlight. Designed and hooked by Anne-Marie Littenberg, Burlington, Vermont. 28" by 47". *Courtesy of Sharon Townsend, Altoona, Iowa.*

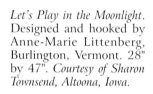

Buckingham. Hooked by Joan Mohrmann, Adirondack, New York". 70" by 46". Designed by Jane McGown Flynn.
"A 25th wedding anniversary gift to my daughter, Melissa, and her husband, Brian, with much love."

Chapter 3

Green Mountain Rug Hooking Guild Recognizes Its Own

This year, our guild chose to honor three very talented rug hooking artists for their achievements in the field of rug hooking. They include Patricia Merikallio from Capitola, California, Michele Micarelli from New Haven, Connecticut, and Emily K. Robertson from Falmouth, Massachusetts. All of these woman have made great contributions to the world of hooked rug making. Not only do their rugs inspire us, they raise the bar for craftsmanship, design, color, imagination, and creativity—surprising and delighting us with their fresh take on a traditional craft. Merikallio, Micarelli, and Robertson are all well-respected rug hooking instructors, encouraging both beginners and experienced rug makers by their own example and through their innovative ideas and workshops. Loved by their students, these three honorees help to keep rug hooking alive, vibrant, and enticing.

Since they are admired and respected equally, the only fair way to present our honorees is to list them alphabetically. Thus we will start with Patricia Merikallio here, then feature Michele Micarelli and Emily K. Robertson in the companion volume to this two volume set. We are proud to recognize all three of these outstanding guild members, and to celebrate their achievements and artistry.

Patricia Merikallio – Guild Honoree 2006

"I started rug hooking when a friend of mine wanted to start teaching, and I became seriously hooked right from the start. That was about twenty-eight years ago. Rug hooking has been my savior for all these years, keeping me almost sane during the raising of three children, the loss of my husband, and the culture shock of moving from the East Coast to the West."

"I went to Wellesley College for two years and then transferred to Parson's School of Design, where I studied fashion design. I worked in the field until I was married, but didn't get back to work until my kids were pretty well-grown, when I got a job with a small sportswear company. The boss was always telling me that a design was great but he didn't know if it would sell, so that was a big impetus for me to start designing my own rugs...they didn't have to please anyone but me and they sure didn't have to sell. From the beginning I loved working with color most, and learned to dye because no one would dye the strong color I wanted. After color came the design. I loved doing borders even before I met rug hooker Jule Marie Smith, although she has surely helped me with them over the years. A lot of ideas for rugs come to me from challenges such as 'A Self-Portrait,' 'A Myth,' and 'In the Garden.' "

"My work has been in two juried shows, at the Wenham Museum and at the Cahoon Museum where I was awarded first place. I've also been featured in two of Jessie Turbayne's books, *Hooked Rugs* and *Hooked Rug Treasury*. In addition, my work has been in *Rug Hooking* magazine and *Celebrations*. Right now I live in a little town on Monterey Bay in California near two of my children and five grandchildren. I've told them that it was time I became a burden to them, but I seriously hope that doesn't happen any time soon."

—Pat Merikallio

A whimsical sign hand painted by rug show co-chair Rae Harrell welcomes show visitors to Patricia Merikallio's inviting section of the exhibition.

Honoree Patricia Merikallio at the opening reception, March 31, 2006. The Round Barn, Shelburne Museum.

Sea Otters. Designed and hooked by Patricia Merikallio, Capitola, California. 26" by 36". *Courtesy of the Merikallio-Conley family, Aptos, California.*

"This is a rug for my twin grandchildren. They live in a town on Monterey Bay where these animals live. Around the border are all the creatures that the otters eat. They wind the kelp around themselves so they won't drift out to sea."

Young Mermaid With Her Catfish. Designed and hooked by Patricia Merikallio, Capitola, California. 31" by 37". "I hooked this rug to enter a competition called 'Hooked on the Sea' held at the Cahoon Museum on Cape Cod. The top half of the mermaid is from a painting by Amzi Phillips, and her tail is by another early American painter, Mary Ann Willson. The rug won first place!"

Max and Sushi. Designed and hooked by Patricia Merikallio, Capitola, California. 25" by 41". "Max, Fritz's less glamorous brother, was always a wimpy cat, so I decided to make him 'heroic' by picturing him too big for the picture, and I had him dreaming of tropical fish."

Fritz's Fantasy. Designed and hooked by Patricia Merikallio, Capitola, California. 34" by 43". "Fritz was an indoor cat who spent hours on the windowsill bird watching. All the birds in the border (except the rooster and the parrot) were favorite characters in his daily 'Kitty Cat TV' program."

Sam. Designed and hooked by Patricia Merikallio, Capitola, California. 38" by 30". *Courtesy of the Merikallio-Conley family, Aptos, California.*
"This is a portrait of one of the twins. My son took a photo of Sam on a friend's horse and I loved the yellow hat, the proud expression on his face, and the long evening shadows."

Pegasus. Designed and hooked by Patricia Merikallio, Capitola, California. 40" by 44". *Courtesy of the Scott family, Aptos, California.*
"This is another Grandmother rug, this one for Alex, my oldest granddaughter. She requested Pegasus and she wanted his mother, Medusa, too. I tried hard to not make Medusa too scary."

In My Garden. Designed and hooked by Patricia Merikallio, Capitola, California. 28" by 34".
"I did this rug for the Shelburne challenge when the rug show theme was 'In The Garden,' and it shows just where my garden was."

Trick or Treat. Designed and hooked by Patricia Merikallio, Capitola, California. 24" by 20".
"This rug was for the exchange Marilyn Bottjer arranged with Japan. We were to do holidays so I picked Halloween. The cat's name is Fred, and I'm afraid I have enough stuff in this tiny rug for five more, but it was fun to do."

Lion. Designed and hooked by Patricia Merikallio, Capitola, California. 44" by 52". *Courtesy of the Scott family, Aptos, California.* "I designed this rug for Ben, my second grandchild, and the lion scared him to death. We gave this rug to his little brother, and gave Ben his sister's fox rug, and all was well. I used yarn for the lion's mane, and strips of upholstery fabric to outline the leaves in the border."

Benjamin. Designed and hooked by Patricia Merikallio, Capitola, California. 32" by 44". *Courtesy of Phyllis Merikallio Ford, Kittery Point, Maine.* "This rug was my second original-design rug. I was in my 'primitive period' and poor Benjamin looks as if he has on striped pajamas."

Alexandra and Stuart. Designed and hooked by Patricia Merikallio, Capitola, California. 52" by 42". *Courtesy of the Scott family, Aptos, California.*
"I adapted this design from a painting done in 1810. I used my granddaughter's face (awake, not asleep), and I added her cat, Stuart, and a hooked rug under her chair."

Ben. Designed and hooked by Patricia Merikallio, Capitola, California. 52" by 44". *Courtesy of the Scott family, Aptos, California.*
"I did this portrait of Ben from three photos. It was challenging but I like the way the sand came out, and I loved using the wool strips of like value to do it."

Katie. Designed and hooked by Patricia Merikallio, Capitola, California. 38" by 30". *Courtesy of the Merikallio-Conley family, Aptos, California.*
"This is a portrait of Katie, the other half of the twins. I dressed her in Early American clothes and gave her an 18th century doll and a 21st century one. Actually, she loves all creatures more than dolls, snails being one of them, so I gave her symbolic snails in the border."

The Almost Virgin Queen. Designed and hooked by Patricia Merikallio, Capitola, California. 40" by 34". *Courtesy of Phyllis Merikallio Ford, Kittery Point, Maine.*
"I did this rug for the Shelburne rug show challenge of doing a self-portrait. There was no way I was going to do myself nude, so when I saw a new biography of Queen Elizabeth I in the library I had my 'ah-ha' moment. I put my face on her and gave her my hook and hooking bag, but unhappily, the jewels are all hers."

Flying Flowers. Designed and hooked by Patricia Merikallio, Capitola, California. 25" by 34".
"I designed this rug for a workshop on mock shading. I had fun doing the plaid border."

Kirsti's Wedding. Designed and hooked by Patricia Merikallio, Capitola, California. 60" by 48". *Courtesy of the Scott family, Aptos, California.*
"Our family worked very hard weeding and planting for the wedding, and the house and garden never looked better. The fireman came a day or two before the wedding to admire our weedy bonfire, and the dog was a neighbor who became our uninvited guest."

Julie's Scrolls. Designed and hooked by Patricia Merikallio, Capitola, California. 29" by 25". *Courtesy of the Merikallio-Conley family, Aptos, California.*
"Jule Marie Smith gave a workshop to our ATHA (Association of Traditional Hooking Artists) chapter on scrolls and drew this pattern on a very generous piece of rug warp. I faithfully learned how to properly do a scroll, but went home and pulled all that out and did my own thing, adding lots of borders around the scrolls."

Tall Ship. Designed and hooked by Patricia Merikallio, Capitola, California. 38" by 46". *Courtesy of Phyllis Merikallio Ford, Kittery Point, Maine.*
"I wanted to hook a clipper ship, but then I got carried away. I had to do above and below the ocean, put in people, our house, an outhouse, some dogs and cats, horses, sheep, a whale, and some fish."

Fox. Designed and hooked by Patricia Merikallio, Capitola, California. 35" by 35". *Courtesy of the Scott family, Aptos, California.* "This was my first Grandmother rug, and I can't remember why a fox, but he's cheerful."

Boris. Designed and hooked by Patricia Merikallio, Capitola, California. 32" by 42". "I had a teacher who told me that I should hook Oriental rugs because they would look nice in my house, but she knew I would never hook one. So I hooked one with Boris on it."

Chapter 4
Strong Women

This year, guild members were invited to make a hooked piece with a special theme in mind. Members love a challenge, stretching their creativity down avenues they might not normally explore. (For an example of this, look at the rugs in Chapter 3 made by Honoree Pat Merikallio, which she credits as being the product of such challenges.) This year's theme was "Strong Women." It evoked many images for our members, with a variety of definitions of the word "strong." As you will see, even the term "woman" was open for interpretation. The challenge took on a life of its own, stirring memories of strong women of the past, celebrating strong women of today, and even recognizing one strong woman of the future.

Strong Women Serve Humanity.
Designed and hooked by Ruth Hennessey, Walworth, New York. 28" by 22".
"Adapted from c.1920 recruiting poster."

Colonial Mandala. Designed and hooked by Robin Amodio, Westport, New York. 28" by 21".
"She may have spun by firelight after tending to the animals, working in the fields, cooking and cleaning during the day. It was her time to dream. Without any conveniences, she had physical as well as spiritual strength. I used my own handspun yarn to bind the edges."

No Hats in School – Self-Portrait. Designed and hooked by Nancy Phillips, North Fayston, Vermont. 36" by 18".
"A former student created a political cartoon for class about the 'No Hat Rule.' Since I love hats, his cartoon portrayed me walking into school with my hat on, oblivious to the sign. The wind-up key idea came from Deanie Pass, whose class I took at Shelburne."

Volga Mamma. Designed and hooked by Virginia Gregg, Falmouth, Massachusetts. 40" by 30".
"This is my friend Tamara at her dacha on the banks of the Volga River, but it also pays homage to all Russian women who, I believe, are the strength and treasure of their country. The Volga is often called 'Mother Russia.' The Russian name in the border is the title of a famous folk song, 'Volga Mamma.'"

All is Well in My World. Hooked by Nancy Howatt Wilson, Amherst, New Hampshire. 16" by 16". Designed by Nancy Howatt Wilson and rug hooking instructor Pam Anfuso.
"I was given a simple outline of a pineapple to hook for a beginner class project. I learned about 'possibility' while designing and hooking the background. In a strong woman's world, 'all is well' because her world is a world of her own creation, of possibilities she has embraced."

Brave Women of Zimbabwe (#1 in Series of 3). Hooked by Susan Mackey, Tinmouth, Vermont. 15" by 15". Design adapted by Susan Mackey from photos taken by Debra Baasch. "Political oppression and corruption has magnified the hardships. This grandmother proudly showed off her grand-daughter in her white dress, in stark contrast to the destitution of her village. Hooked as a gift to Debra Baasch."

Brave Women of Zimbabwe (#2 in Series of 3). Hooked by Susan Mackey, Tinmouth, Vermont. 12" by 15". Design adapted by Susan Mackey from photos taken by Debra Baasch. "Despite inflation of over six hundred percent and severe food shortages, this mother and child dress for church in beautiful outfits, exemplifying the spirit and hope of Zimbabwe."

Brave Women of Zimbabwe (#3 in Series of 3). Hooked by Susan Mackey, Tinmouth, Vermont. 24" by 12". Design adapted by Susan Mackey from photos taken by Debra Baasch. "The devastating AIDS pandemic has infected twenty-five percent of adults and kills 200,000 each month in sub-Saharan Africa. This grandmother has lost all four of her own children to AIDS and her grandson is severely impaired by malnutrition."

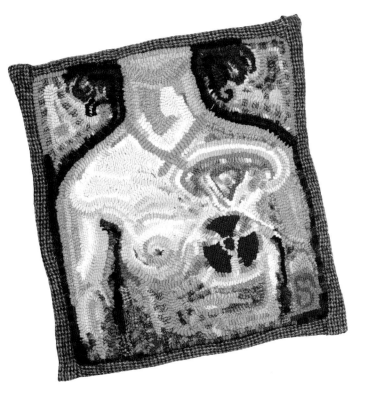

Survivor. Designed and hooked by Carolyn Buttolph of Red House Rugs, St. Johnsbury, Vermont. 16" by 16". "For me, rug hooking is about the freedom you have to hook things your way, the best you can, and it is easier when the subject, like this one, is close to the heart."

The Goddess Within. Designed and hooked by Susie Stephenson, Edgecomb, Maine. 84" by 36". "Within each of us is a beautiful woman with intelligence, strength, beauty, and sexuality. She stays hidden much of the time, but when she gets out, she is unstoppable. Around her are symbols of things that are important to me as a woman."

Pippi Longstocking: The Strongest Girl in the World. Designed and hooked by April P. Simpson, Morrisville, Vermont. 23" by 19". "The most remarkable thing about her was that she was so strong. She was so very strong that in the whole wide world there was not a single police officer as strong as she. Why, she could lift a whole horse if she wanted to!" —Astrid Lindgren, 1950.

Kayaking. Hooked by Nancy L. Brown, Greenland, New Hampshire. 35" by 21". Designed by Beverly Conway Designs.

"I am a kayaker and hooking this rug during the winter gave me a chance to recall the good times I have enjoyed while kayaking during the summer. I am looking forward to seeing it every day on my wall. I liked using fancy novelty yarns for sparkle and a chuckle."

Soul Sister. Designed and hooked by Lynne Fowler, Westover, Maryland. 41" by 28".

"This rug was the result of an encounter with a group of African-American youths on a hot summer day. Their comment really tickled me and I knew I had to do something with it one day."

Put Your Big Girl Panties On. Hooked by Melonie Bushey, Vergennes, Vermont. 33" by 34". Designed by Beverly Conway Designs.

My Turkish Lady. Designed and hooked by Betty Oberstar, Wilton, Connecticut. 36" by 28".
"Several years ago, I was fortunate to join one of Jule Marie Smith's classes on border design. Without her help, I would not have been able to fit this intricate border around my central motif, which was adapted from designs found on 17th century Turkish ceramics."

Strong Women Take Themselves Lightly. Designed and hooked by Barbara Held, Tinmouth, Vermont. 31" by 36".
"I read a young adult book, *Night Flying* by Rita Murphy, which was about a family of women whose secret was that they could fly at night, as a rite of passage into evolved consciousness. It reminded me that we too, as strong women, can 'fly' if we take ourselves lightly and don't get in our own way."

Herself. Designed and hooked by Gail Huff, Victor, New York. 49" by 30".
"Several books about God being a woman inspired this rug. The design incorporates symbols of femininity (snake), wisdom (owl), self-discovery (labyrinth), and Mother Earth. This design was an opportunity for me to try using embellishments (metallic ribbon, needle felting, beading, fibers, and metallic trim) for the first time."

NY Chic. Designed and hooked by Molly W. Dye, Jacksonville, Vermont. 29" by 18".
"The show will go on. All across America from city to small town the strong women of theater and show business are a tribute to the strength of our society."

When I Am Old. Designed and hooked by Janice Peyton, Excello, Missouri. 25" by 21".
"A tribute to my mom, Thelma Hull (1916-2001), the quintessential red hat lady. An earring in her bellybutton is stretching her horizons, possibly the blue jeans, but who knows, she's special, as the heart in the corner depicts. Thanks to Rae Harrell for the inspiration."

Pam & Burt. Hooked by Shirley Wiedemann, East Falmouth, Massachusetts. 19" by 25". Designed by Shirley Wiedemann and drawn by Jon Ciemiewicz.
"This piece was from a photograph of my niece, Pam, who is an accomplished equestrian. Pam has her own riding school in Pennsylvania and shows many kinds of strength, both inner and physical."

Tomorrow Will Be a Better Day. Designed and hooked by Rachelle LeBlanc, Ste-Julie, Quebec, Canada. 33" by 39". "Living through a burnout. This rug was done when all I wanted to do was sleep. Now going through and overcoming depression, this rug is a reminder of my strength."

Strong Women Then, Strong Women Now. Designed and hooked by Joyce B. Elmore, Huntington, Vermont. 28" by 10".
"The 'strong women' theme of this year's rug show reminds me of the cadet student nurses then, and the nurses of today. I have met, admired, and worked with these women for over fifty years."

Emma, Going to the River. Hooked by Edith McClure, Farmington, Connecticut. 28" by 34". Designed by Elizabeth Black.
"Emma is her own person. Here she is at her favorite place, waiting to chase a stick into the river. Emma is strong and assertive."

Grandma. Designed and hooked by Judy Coolidge, Pawlet, Vermont. 17" by 12". "I designed this as a tribute to my great-grandmother, Jessie Dawson Harrington from Danby, Vermont (February 1863 - March 1943). She was a 'strong woman,' nurse, teacher, mother, and grandmother, who could claim eighty-eight living descendants at the time of her death. Today there are hundreds living because she lived."

Cecelia P. Wenski. Designed and hooked by Denise W. Jose, Keuka Park, New York. 26" by 24". "This rug is a picture of my mother. As the years go by, I realize just how strong she really was."

Shaker Woman. Designed and hooked by Milda Peake, Brattleboro, Vermont. 16" diameter. "I have always been inspired by the Shaker people."

Ms. Gourdie. Hooked by Karen Quigley, Vergennes, Vermont. 30" by 14". Designed by Breezy Ridge Rugs. "Ms. Gourdie is the queen of the garden. She oversees all the vegetables and wants everyone to know that she is more than a fall table decoration. Her cat keeps the vermin away as well."

Arizona Spirit. Designed and hooked by Angela Foote, Barrington, New Hampshire. 27" by 23".
" 'Arizona Spirit' represents the dramatic color palette of the southwest rising up through the human spirit."

Nettie. Hooked by Carol Munson, Sunderland, Vermont. 16" by 16". Design adapted by Sue Janssen from the drawings of Elaine Dixon.
"Nettie Stevens (1861-1912) was one of the first female scientists to make a name for herself in the biological sciences. She was born in Cavendish, Vermont. She and my mother share last names, no relation however."

Clarina Nichols: An Awesome Vermont Woman. Hooked by Elizabeth Morgan, Wallingford, Vermont. 17" by 17". Design adapted by Sue Janssen from the drawings of Elaine Dixon.
"Sue Janssen inspired and challenged me to join her in punch hooking a silhouette of one of the 'Eleven Awesome Vermont Women' drawings by Elaine Dixon. Clarina Nichols (1810-1885) was the first woman in Vermont and Kansas to secure property rights for women."

Lucy Wheelock: An Awesome Vermont Woman. Hooked by Sue Janssen, Benson, Vermont. 17" by 17". Design adapted by Sue Janssen from the drawings of Elaine Dixon.
"Lots of inspiration here! Amy Oxford, Elizabeth Morgan, and my mom inspired me to try my first punch hooking. Elaine Dixon's drawings for 'Eleven Awesome Vermont Women' inspired this hanging—and then there's Lucy Wheelock (1857-1946), a Vermont woman who spent sixty years teaching kindergarten and training others to teach!"

Backyard Matriarchy. Designed and hooked by Victoria Lowell, Falmouth, Massachusetts. 25" by 24".
"Our son is a third generation beekeeper. Worker bees (sexually undeveloped females) are the hive labor force. His wife keeps chickens, but no rooster. A seemingly lonely wild hen turkey has lurked outside the coop. Affection for this assemblage of strong 'women' and for their keepers inspired my rug."

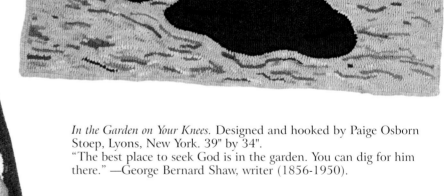

Women – Strength Through Loving Friendships. Designed and hooked by Sunnie Andress of Old Crow Farm, Newport, Vermont. 19" by 19".
"This rug was such fun to design and hook. I wanted to illustrate the love and emotional strength women friends give to each other. I also wanted to present the female friends in a whimsical way with a symbolic 'rainy day' background."

In the Garden on Your Knees. Designed and hooked by Paige Osborn Stoep, Lyons, New York. 39" by 34".
"The best place to seek God is in the garden. You can dig for him there." —George Bernard Shaw, writer (1856-1950).

Sisters. Designed and hooked by Jennifer Grahovac, North Middlesex, Vermont. 28" by 38".
"My sisters and I made one last visit to the family farm after it was sold. We climbed into the hayloft and looked out at the farm and talked about all our childhood memories there. My husband snapped a photo of us as we reminisced."

Waiting for the Parade. Designed and hooked by Rachelle LeBlanc, Ste-Julie, Quebec, Canada. 38" by 45".
"This rug was inspired by a black and white photograph of my Acadian grandmother. She was beautiful and smart. I never had a chance to meet her, but people still talk about what a wonderful person she was."

Adam and Eve and Pinchme. Hooked by Ann Hallett, Coldwater, Ontario, Lokieo, Canada. 21" by 52". Adapted from original artwork by Emily Carr, Rittermere-Hurst-Field.
"Went down to the river to bathe. Who do you think was saved?"

My Mentors. Designed and hooked by Diane S. Learmonth, Anacortes, Washington. 16" by 31".
"From left to right: Sharon Townsend, Dori Byers, and Lois Egenes. Three of the dearest, kindest, wisest strong women I know. They are what I aspire to someday."

Ginkgoes and Grammys. Designed and hooked by Sharon Townsend, Altoona, Iowa. 29" by 20".
"We have three generations of grandmothers in our family. Like the ginkgo leaves, they are in different stages of their lives but all have wisdom."

Salute to Emily Dickinson. Designed and hooked by Ivi Nelson Collier, Nottingham, Maryland. 23" by 18".
"Temperament and illness kept poet Emily Dickinson close to home in Amherst, Massachusetts. Inspiration for this rug came as I stood in the austere white bedroom where she wrote. I imagined Emily reentering the house from the garden she loved and realized her room was not austere at all."

Three Headstrong Women. Designed and hooked by Jeri Laskowski, Rochester, New York. 27" by 22".
"Attempts at hooking faces have frustrated me. Using simplified cartoon-like faces similar to those seen in Roussillon, France, I felt was more successful. Red hair seemed an appropriate choice since Roussillon is noted for its architecture in numerous shades of red and a local ochre quarry."

Oregon or Bust. Designed and hooked by Darcy Cardas, Bandon, Oregon. 19" by 25".
"While driving across Eastern Oregon, Montana, and South Dakota it was so long, sometimes boring, with difficult landscapes. I imagined how strong one needed to be to walk this every day."

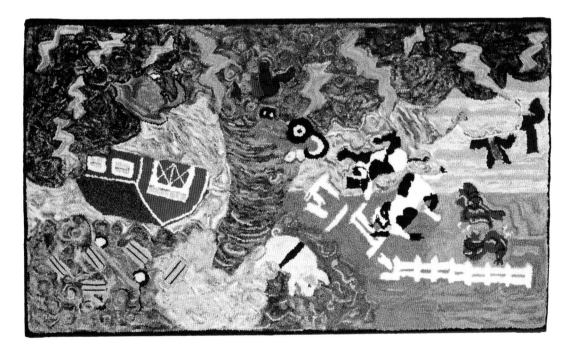

Mother Nature. Designed and hooked by Julie Robinson, Loudon, New Hampshire. 24" by 40".
"Mother Nature, with all her fury. She matches up to the strongest of women. With all of the natural disasters this past year, I felt she earned her place among strong women."

Lady Colleen. Designed and hooked by Susan Alain, Montreal, Quebec, Canada. 27" by 33".
"This is a rug I made for my friends the Finck family. Charlie (C) the father, was born in the lighthouse on the island behind the boat. He and son Paul (P), are owners of *The Lady Colleen,* named after Colleen, Charlie's daughter (Paul's sister), who died of breast cancer at age fifty-one. Her name is hooked in her handwriting. Beatrice (B), is Charlie's wife and she holds the whole thing up."

When you're a rug hooker, inspiration is everywhere. Sometimes it comes from grand things, like the paintings of the masters, or Vermont's breathtaking vistas. Other times inspiration is found in the small, more humble details of everyday life. While many people might pass these things by, to a rug hooker they can be a jumping off point, leading to the creation of the next rug (or saved for future use). The following two rugs from the show are wonderful examples of this. Each was inspired by a tiny scrap of paper that offered sage advice in eight words or less...

Strong Spirit. Designed and hooked by Jane Griswold, Rutland, Vermont. 30" by 20".
"This hanging was inspired by a tea bag tag. I have carried the tag for twenty-one years."

Spirit of Adventure. Designed and hooked by Sherillee Baker, Winterport, Maine. 22" by 29".
"When the theme for this year's show was announced, I knew that I wanted to hook something that captured my exciting experience kayaking on the North Atlantic. But...not until I received a fortune cookie with this inside did the entire concept get formulated: 'Let the spirit of adventure set the tone.' "

Grandma's Cottage. Hooked by Linda L. Smith, Fair Haven, Vermont. 25" by 21". Designed by Rittermere-Hurst-Field. "This rug is in memory of my grandma who was a strong and courageous woman. She came to this country from Canada and taught herself English. She raised sixteen children and lived to be ninety-eight. I can still see her baking pies and playing cards with me."

Athena. Designed and hooked by Helena G. Rice, Plainfield, Vermont. 21" by 28".
"Athena is the Greek Goddess of wisdom, weaving, and textiles. She is a horse tamer and the patron of Athens, olive trees, and cultivation. Daughter of Zeus, she fends off enemies with secrets of lightning and the power of the Gorgon. Athena represents strength of women; she is the embodiment of intellect, creativity, and peace through reason."

Crowns. Designed and hooked by Kris McDermet, Dummerston, Vermont. 32" by 42".
"The inspiration for this rug came from reading *The Secret Life of Bees* by Sue Monk Kidd and *Crowns* by Michael Cunningham. Both honor African-American women and their strength, imagination, and commitment to their spiritual life and family."

Mother Earth. Designed and hooked by Julie Robinson, Loudon, New Hampshire. 30" by 29".
"Mother Earth with animals representing each of the seven continents. We all share responsibility in keeping her strong and everlasting."

Run With Scissors. Designed and hooked by Jill Cooper, Riverdale, Georgia. 23" by 20".
"When I became fifty, it was a defining year in my life. The older I get, the more I don't follow 'the rules.' This rug was a way to share my belief that you must take every chance you can to enjoy all the beauty of life."

Bermuda Escape. Hooked by Karen L. Tompson, Standish, Maine. 26" diameter. Designed by Janet Conner.
"Created after my extremely emotionally devastating divorce, this piece symbolizes when I first found the 'strong woman' within myself, allowing me to take my first vacation with girlfriends, make my first hooked rug, and braid my first border."

Berry Bed Rug. Hooked by Eileen M. Friedrich, Groton, Massachusetts. 72" by 52". Designed by George Kahnle for Hooked on the Creek.
"Who is Lydia? Ancestral grandmother, Lydia Howe, eighteen, married Wm. Whitaker, Minuteman, in 1774. I hooked this bed rug for her. Throughout the process, her spirit always guided my hook and choice of colors. I know she is pleased."

One Egg? Hooked by Karen Detrick, New Lexington, Ohio. 35" by 48". Designed by Melody Hoops, Fleecewood Farms Designs.

"Melody Hoops was 'doodling' with some farm ideas and borrowed a book of antique advertising tins for ideas. Here are the results: 'One Egg?' This strong woman's strength and power translate into the skillet or the stew pot."

Study of Rouault's "Arlequin." Designed and hooked by Noriko Manago, Kumano-shi, Japan. 17" by 12".

"In Diane Phillips' class, we studied the face. I chose Rouault's 'Arlequin' as a strong 'woman.' In her sorrowful gaze, can't we see her lust for life?"

Family Tree of Aurore Pepin. Hooked by Dianne Pepin, Laconia, New Hampshire. 33" by 44". Designed by Pris Buttler Rug Designs.

"Aurore is the tree. The life and fruit of this tree began with her. The dark berries are her five children; the clusters are the families they created. Each berry grows from the stem of its parent and gets lighter in shade with the next generation. The two hearts in the light gold background are my brother's foster children and my aunt's step-grandsons, The circles in the background represent the spirit of ancestors and children yet to come."

Matriarch. Designed and hooked by Eunice Whitney Heinlein, Avon, Connecticut. 22" by 22".

Self-Portrait. Designed and hooked by Suzanne Kowalski, South Burlington, Vermont. 14" diameter.
"My self-portrait was done in a June 2005 workshop at Rae Harrell's. I used the greens because I had once taken an oil portrait class and green was used as an under painting."

Katharine. Designed and hooked by Barbara Held, Tinmouth, Vermont. 16" by 15".
"I was inspired by Katharine Hepburn's quote, 'As one goes through life one learns that if you don't paddle your own canoe you don't move.' It reminds me that I am responsible for who and what I am, and it gives me great courage."

Self-Portrait. Hooked by Liz Alpert Fay, Sandy Hook, Connecticut. 18" by 12". Designed by Liz Alpert Fay in class with Rae Harrell.
"This piece was created in a self-portrait class with Rae Harrell."

Chloe. Designed and hooked by Jule Marie Smith, Ballston Spa, New York. 16" by 13". "I wanted to hook this face in multicolor. I loved working with the hair in pools of dark. And I so enjoy the strong contrast. I had a lot of fun making it. I've been in a brighter color, stronger contrast phase."

Once Strong, Now Alzheimer's. Designed and hooked by Diane Kelly, Dorset, Vermont. 21" by 19". "This rug is my idea of what it must be like to suffer from Alzheimer's Disease: to be shut away from the joy and beauty of the world around you."

Ruthie Elizabeth Smith. Designed and hooked by Jule Marie Smith, Ballston Spa, New York. 15" by 14". "This is a likeness of my granddaughter, Ruthie, truly a budding strong woman at eighteen months. My inspiration was Mary Cassatt and perhaps the background was most successful!"

Dreaming of Blue Skies (Triptych). Designed and hooked by Diane Phillips, Fairport, New York. Left and right face 14" by 14", center face 14" by 16".
"For each workshop on 'Faces' that I do, I hook a face as a demonstration. I use the same face, but make each woman different in some way. This triptych represents three of my favorites, an Arab woman (left), an African woman (center), and a battered woman (right), all dreaming of blue skies."

Refugee Girl. Designed and hooked by Sara Judith, Nelson, British Colombia, Canada. 15" by 15".
"We cannot possibly appreciate the plight of the world's refugees, particularly the women who must try to keep their households and families together. I also believe we all have largely untapped reserves of strength. These women have to access their strengths every day in their precarious existence."

I Don't Think So. Designed and hooked by Cathy Henning, Burlington, Ontario, Canada. 18" by 17". "This is the result of playing with the spacing rules for facial features and adapting a slight off center effect to create one ear I needed for my one pearl button. The hair is my idea of the current hair design."

Self-Portrait. Designed and hooked by Maureen Yates, South Burlington, Vermont. 16" by 15". "I took Rae Harrell's face class last summer. It was a wonderful two days. Rae is a very nurturing teacher."

Self-Portrait. Designed and hooked by Kristina Burnett, Canaan, New Hampshire. 25" by 16". "I was fortunate last summer to have a week alone on the coast of Maine. Before I arrived I gave a lot of thought to a self-portrait in wool and planned it carefully in my mind's eye. Once in Maine I hooked it in four short days. Solitude is a wonderful thing."

49

Louise. Designed and hooked by Kathleen Menzies, Greenfield Park, Quebec, Canada. 3.75" by 4".
"This is a portrait of my mother. She was a fun-loving woman who had a great sense of humor. She made us laugh and made life fun for us when we were younger. Miniature rug hooking."

Strong Women Reach for the Stars. Designed and hooked by Carol Morris Petillo, Vinalhaven, Maine. 32" by 32".
"This rug began as an experiment in Rae Harrell's 2005 class. I came home with my face, one star, a drawing by Rae of an outstretched arm, and the theme for this year's show. This rug is the result."

N.Y. VIA IA. Designed and hooked by Diane S. Learmonth, Anacortes, Washington. 27" by 26".
"A self-portrait. I grew up in western New York, on Lake Ontario. For the last seven years we have lived in Iowa, the land of corn and soybeans. Very little water and not a happy girl...Rae Harrell was my teacher."

Susan. Designed and hooked by Jule Marie Smith, Ballston Spa, New York. 23" by 21".
"I had been thinking about faces with a twist and the black-eyed Susan came to mind. The dark colors were challenging and fun and so enhanced by the yellow petals. The background squares in face colors made the rug more unique."

Leda & the Swan, Do-Over. Designed and hooked by Ivi Nelson Collier, Nottingham, Maryland. 26" by 20".
"In ancient myth and the poem by Yeats, a god assumes the form of a swan and ravishes Leda. In my version, the tables are turned and Leda not only wins the tussle, she gains a gorgeous hat and earrings."

Self-Portrait. Designed and hooked by Constance Frost, Hinesburg, Vermont. 23" by 18".

Fruits of the Earth. Hooked by Jan Hammond, Indianapolis, Indiana. 13" by 13". Design adapted by Jan Hammond from a pattern by The House of Price, Inc.
"Using a basket of leftover strips this face came into play. What fun this was to do."

Medicine Woman/Spirit Talker. Designed and hooked by Jon Ciemiewicz, Litchfield, New Hampshire. 20" by 20". "Spiritually the strongest woman in a Native American tribe, she carried the weight of the tribe's issues on her shoulders."

Self-Portrait. Designed and hooked by Mary Hulette, South Burlington, Vermont. 17" by 17".
"I did this during a faces class I took with Rae Harrell at her home last summer. My daughter thinks it looks like me; my husband is not so sure. I'm wearing my backpack—for the journey—and I have my stars to guide me."

Self-Portrait. Hooked by Diane Burgess, Hinesburg, Vermont. 19" by 18". Designed by Diane Burgess, as taught by Rae Harrell. "Inspiration from taking Rae Harrell's workshop with my Hinesburg hooking friends at Rae's home."

Lydia, the Tattooed Lady. Designed and hooked by Karen Baxter Cooper, New London, New Hampshire. 19" by 18".
"Rae Harrell taught us a face formula in class at Shelburne 2005. The result, a bit fierce, called for creative naming—hence 'Lydia, the Tattooed Lady,' a woman strong enough to bare history on her skin."

If You Knew "Susan." Designed and hooked by Shirley Zandy, Tinmouth, Vermont. 21" by 19".
"While thinking about just who I thought could be called a 'strong woman,' Susan instantly came to mind. The title says it all. I've known Susan for many years, and if faced with only half of what she has endured, I hope that I should have her strength, courage, and wisdom."

All the Things I Have to Do! Designed and hooked by Lesa Morrissey, Hampton, New Hampshire. 24" by 36".
"As a single woman, I'm constantly trying to remember all the things I have to do—my mind is chock full!"

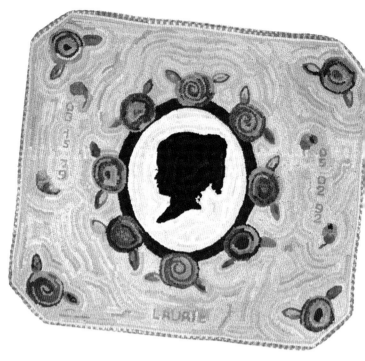

Laurie. Designed and hooked by Stephanie Gibson, St. Clairsville, Ohio. 32" by 37".
"Loss and grief is a human experience. This rug not only honors the memory of my daughter, Laurie, but is a tribute and a prayer to all those who live this experience every day."

Self-Portrait – Rae Says. Hooked by Patt Weimer, Danielson, Connecticut. 28" by 25". Designed by Patt Weimer of Noah's Wife Designs.
"2005 class with Rae Harrell at Region I – Madison, Connecticut. Doesn't look like me, but everyone recognized the jewelry. 'I am the girl who has the curl in the middle of my forehead, when I'm good I'm very good, when I'm bad I'm better.' "

Susie-Ecologist-1971. Designed and hooked by Susan Leskin, West Burke, Vermont. 25" by 22".
"This self-portrait represents a time in my life when I was most hopeful, proud, full of energy and spirit. I have devoted my life to biology, conservation, healthcare and creating landscapes for people and animals. My roots are in the earth."

Afternoon in Provence. Designed and hooked by Diane Phillips, Fairport, New York. 42" by 36". "I've been studying the impressionists for several years, particularly the way they used color. With this piece I wanted to play with strong colors in the figure and the flowers. I wanted the work to appear spontaneous and to have a French flair."

High Priestess. Designed and hooked by Michele Velez, Hamden, Connecticut. 24" by 18". "This rug was hooked and designed in a class with Rae Harrell. It was inspired by my love of all things magical, mysterious, and Egyptian."

Judith. Designed and hooked by Judith Dallegret, Montreal, Quebec, Canada. 27" by 27". "This 'Judith' rug was hooked to honor several women of tremendous strength and courage: Judy Chicago, creator of the amazing 'Dinner Party' in the 1970s; Judith from the Bible; Artemisia Gentileschi, who painted the remarkable 'Judith Slaying of Holofernes' in 1613, and my own self portrait!"

55

Still Winning. Designed and hooked by Sharon Townsend, Altoona, Iowa. 46" by 38".

"Two days after surgery for a perforated ulcer, Mother, at ninety-one, was sitting in a bedside chair playing cards. Now that's a strong woman. The side borders are a 1913 textile pattern, the year she was born."

Lady Liberty Speaks. Designed and hooked by Barbara Held, Tinmouth, Vermont. 25" by 17". "Lady Liberty was originally designed for the American Folk Art Museum's 'Icons of America' contest. I wanted to show, as a reminder to us all, that our country was based on freedom, justice, and liberty for all people. Lady Liberty is truly a 'strong women.' "

Angel Queen – Fraktur Style. Hooked by Janet Myette, Glens Falls, New York. 25" by 36". Designed by George Kahnle for Hooked on the Creek.

"This rug was so much fun to do that I also did a miniature punch needle version of it (see page 153). With the help of my great teacher, Dick LaBarge, I was able to color plan both of these beautiful rugs."

Fran Angel. Hooked by Mary Gebhardt, Milford, Connecticut. 10" by 32". Designed by Mary Gebhardt in class with Diane Phillips.
"Fighting breast cancer in 1966 (and for the next thirty-seven years) left a woman permanently disfigured, physically and emotionally. But it also made my mother a very strong woman. She is my hero and the angel that guards my home."

Tribute. Hooked by Dinah Cutting, Andover, Maine. 20" by 34". Designed by Tina Payton.
"Tina had designed and hooked this rug as a memorial to her mother. I wanted to do the same as a memorial for my daughter, Mindy. This is my first rug, but not my last!"

Susan, Happy On E. Ironbound. Designed and hooked by Susan Alain, Montreal, Quebec, Canada. 21" by 25".
"Started in Rae Harrell's 2004 class, this rug ended up quite differently than originally planned. I was interested in hooking dark on dark."

Leiana. Designed and hooked by Lynne Fowler, Westover, Maryland. 33" by 26".

"One of the strongest young women that I know is my daughter Liana Grasso (Leiana is her stage name). She is bravely facing incredible challenges to achieve her goal."

Pele – Goddess of Hawaii's Volcanoes. Hooked by Layne G. Herschel, Chester, Vermont. 37" by 37". Design adapted by Layne G. Herschel from the artwork of Herb Kawainui Kane as featured in his book, *Pele – Goddess of Hawaii's Volcanoes*.

"On a trip to Hawaii with my sister, Dana, I was awed by the magnificence and spirituality of the volcanoes. This rug depicts Pele-honua-mea of the sacred land. Eater of land when she devours the land with her flames."

Swimming With the Sharks. Designed and hooked by Sara Judith, Nelson, British Colombia, Canada. 25" by 27".

"A strong powerful woman swimming, adapted from the picture 'Whale' by Rachael Field. Then a class by Laurie Wiles opened possibilities of using other fibers. A glitzy bathing suit, silk seaweed, and wild mohair hair resulted. What was planned as a bathmat (terry cloth for arms and legs) was lifted off the floor!"

Chapter 5

Orientals

Song of Persia. Hooked by Carol T. Dale, Gilford, New Hampshire. 36" by 58". Designed by Jane McGown Flynn.
"I wanted to hook an Oriental pattern in an unusual color scheme. I dyed all the wools and worked on the rug for six years."

Kilim Pillow. Hooked by Tony Latham, Montreal, Quebec, Canada. 16" by 16". Traditional design adapted by Tony Latham. "I love the flat weaves. Great opportunity to play with color. Fun geometric designs."

Tibetan Dragons. Hooked by Laura W. Pierce, Petaluma, California. 22" by 22". Design adapted from a Tibetan textile by Laura W. Pierce. "After visiting a Tibetan art show at the Asian Art Museum in San Francisco, I was inspired to hook a small Oriental design. I wanted to show my students how to use a spot dye. The red border consists of five different red skirts."

A Version of Persian. Designed and hooked by Lara Magruder, Hayward, California. 44" by 32".

Charity. Hooked by Tricia Tague Miller,
Alstead, New Hampshire. 23" by 38".
Designed by Jane McGown Flynn.

Early Persia. Hooked by Eunice
Whitney Heinlein, Avon, Con-
necticut. 43" by 28". Designed by
Jane McGown Flynn.

61

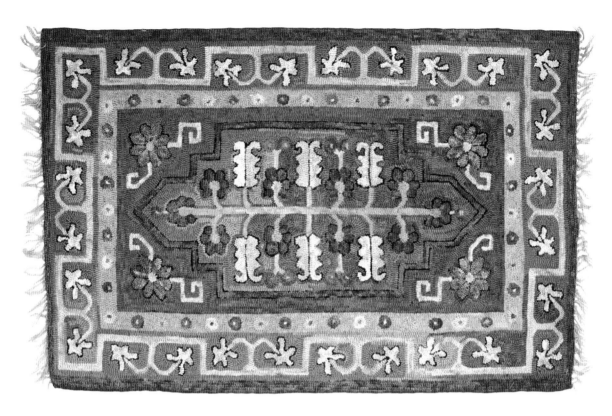

Khotan. Hooked by Darcy Cardas, Bandon, Oregon. 28" by 44". Designed by Jane McGown Flynn.
"The color plan for this rug was inspired by an old rug that had pomegranates on the center tree. I enjoy hooking wide strips and the challenge to dye for this rather than use swatches for fine shading."

Turkish Tradition. Hooked by Devin Ryder, Somerville, Massachusetts. 24" by 37". Designed by Jane McGown Flynn.
"There is something about angular Oriental designs that I absolutely love. I wanted this rug to have the colors of a moss agate."

Beshir. Hooked by Sheila M. Breton, Surry, New Hampshire. 14" by 22". Designed by Jane McGown Flynn.

Petite Persian. Hooked by Gail Majauckas, West Newbury, Massachusetts. 36" by 28". Designed by New Earth Designs. "My first (and last) Oriental! Used up a lot of 'accidentally' dyed wool in this one!"

Kilim – Oriental. Hooked by Dick LaBarge, Victory Mills, New York. 30" by 21". Designed by The House of Price, Inc.

Chapter 6
Florals

Ever since the first rug makers took up their hooks, flowers have been one of their favorite subjects. Always a popular and well-represented category in our show, floral rugs are particularly loved by hooked rug makers for their adaptability. There are so many ways to hook a poppy, an iris, or even a dandelion. They can be made to look so realistic you can almost watch them grow, or so fanciful that their species is uncertain. Famous rug hooker Pearl K. McGown even made up a name for unknown flowers that were created from our imaginations. She called them "padulas."

What is it that makes blossoms, blooms, berries, and buds such a passion? Is it the fact that we just plain love real live flowers and want to capture their beauty? Or, is it that they can be such a fun challenge? Perhaps we love them so because they are very accommodating, allowing us to create our own natural world with our own self-styled "padulas." Is it the joy of capturing summer to savor over the long bleak winters? Or maybe it's the fact that, unlike certain other two-legged and four-legged subjects, plants are so good at holding still when they pose for us. Whatever the reasons, florals are cheerful to have in the house. If you pay attention, you can almost smell their fragrance as your feet shuffle across their pile.

All floral rugs from the exhibit are included here, except for any rugs depicting flower baskets and fruit. Those two groups will be featured in this book's companion volume.

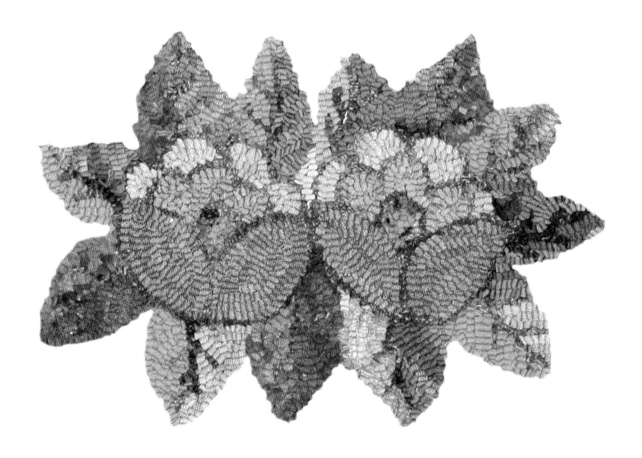

Mamouth. Hooked by Sarah Guiliani, South Portland, Maine. 38" by 52". Designed by Patsy Becker.
"I love the design and my colors. Goes great in my home. Done with a #8 cut."

Hollyhocks. Designed and
hooked by Marcia Kent,
Wilmington, Massachusetts.
28" by 24".
"A flower so stately, luscious,
and bright, with memories of a
long ago garden."

The Red Rug. Designed and hooked by Nancy Z. Parcels, Mechanicsburg, Pennsylvania. 28" by 40". "The inspiration for this rug came from an old Pennsylvania Dutch painted trunk. The simple design comes alive by the movement in the wool. The background is many grays overdyed with red."

Berries Underfoot. Hooked by Nell Berntsen, Acworth, New Hampshire. 24" by 18". Designed by Patsy Becker. "I wanted to use this great plaid we had at the store where I work to hook the berries."

Bouquet of Pink. Hooked by Maureen Rowe, Dollard-Des-Ormeaux, Quebec, Canada. 19" diameter. Design created during a shading workshop with flowers adapted from the book *Shading Flowers*, by Jeanne Field.
"Pink is one of my favorite colors. So a bouquet of pink flowers is one of my favorite things in all the world."

Hellebores. Designed and hooked by Claudia Van Nes, Chester, Connecticut. 36" by 24".
"I started rug hooking in the fall of 2005, when guild member Marilyn Sly kindly introduced me to it. This is my first rug; the design derived from a flower I love. I'm hooked now."

The Helen Rug. Hooked by Priscilla Buzzell, Newport, Vermont. 29" by 18". Design adapted by Helen Wolfel from a very old pattern.
"This little rug is a favorite among Helen's students and friends. Someday we shall have an exhibit of the many colors we all put into this rug."

A Secret Garden. Hooked by Nancy Bachand, Vergennes, Vermont. 31" by 32". Designed by Karen Kahle and Primitive Spirit.

A Secret Garden. Hooked by Karyn Lord, Plymouth, Massachusetts. 31" by 31". Designed by Karen Kahle and Primitive Spirit.
"This has been my favorite rug to hook and I was almost sad to finish it! I started 'A Secret Garden' in a workshop taught by Karen Kahle in 2004, and I truly felt like a painter while working on this rug."

Floral Leaf Fantasy. Hooked by Carole Mielke, Montpelier, Vermont. 51" by 27". Designed by Green Mountain Patterns.

Sandringham. Hooked by Amy Spokes, South Burlington, Vermont. 35" by 24". Designed by Joan Moshimer. "The crewel design intrigued me but I wanted to use brighter colors on a dark background rather than the more muted colors on light backgrounds used in 'real' crewel work. The border required several tries with various color combinations, and consultations with the Richmond group."

In Spite of You! Designed and hooked by Jane Perry, Shelburne, Vermont. 30" by 21". "Beautiful gardens can be created in spite of dandelions! Dick LaBarge and George Kahnle created the climate for my design; my hooking colleagues added inspiration."

Coneflower Border. Designed and hooked by Diane Gage, Akron, Pennsylvania. 22" by 33".
"I wanted to design a rug in which the predominant feature was the border. My husband had been petitioning for a coneflower themed rug for quite some time and his input was incredibly helpful."

Untitled. Hooked by Mary Sargent, Johnson, Vermont. 18" by 27". Designer unknown.
"I arrived at hooking group one day and realized I had my frame, cutter, and wool but had forgotten my rug. After picking out this pattern I chose to do it all in six value swatches. I call this my swatch rug. It is done in mock shading style."

Sunderland Ferns. Designed and hooked by Carol Munson, Sunderland, Vermont. 25" by 44".
"The woods beyond our house are filled with ferns that are depicted on this rug. The rug ferns are true to their forms, the various shades of green I used are not. I uncovered a few forgotten pressed ones under the living room rug after the rug was completed."

Flowered Ferns. Designed and hooked by Kathleen Patten, Hinesburg, Vermont. 64" by 29".
"This rug evolved from my desire to hook with purple and green."

Seth. Hooked by Sara Burghoff, Underhill, Vermont. 42" by 32". A Moxley Design from Green Mountain Patterns.
"Stephanie Krauss' oak leaf design is wonderful. I added the border. I'm not sure it complements the center design. I dyed my own variegated yarn to match my couch. My friend loves the 'blueberries' and gets upset when I tell her they are blue acorns!"

Apothecary Rose. Hooked by Mary Hulette, South Burlington, Vermont. 48" by 34". Designed by Karen Kahle and Primitive Spirit.
"I hooked this rug as a wedding present for Kevin and Carrie Sickles, our dear nephew and his beautiful bride. They were married June 10, 2005 in Marlton, New Jersey."

Antique Rose Runner. Hooked by Lynn Uptmor, Battle Ground, Washington. 53" by 20". Designed by Karen Kahle and Primitive Spirit.

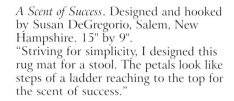

A Scent of Success. Designed and hooked by Susan DeGregorio, Salem, New Hampshire. 15" by 9".
"Striving for simplicity, I designed this rug mat for a stool. The petals look like steps of a ladder reaching to the top for the scent of success."

Maple Leaf Rag Rug. Designed and hooked by Sara Judith, Nelson, British Colombia, Canada. 41" by 24".
"The Canadian flag carries one of the only living symbols on a flag, the maple leaf. I love its relevance to life in Canada. Scattered maple leaves cover a background hooked with the Canadian maple leaf tartan."

71

Pungent Pine. Hooked by Suzanne Dirmaier, Waterbury Center, Vermont. 25" by 35". Designed by Heirloom Rugs. "I love the old fashioned campy feel of pine patterns. So when this pattern came up at an ATHA (Association of Traditional Hooking Artists) auction I jumped on it. It had been started, but thank God for Dorr swatches. It's going to live at our cottage on the lake."

Mighty Oak. Hooked by Kathleen Harwood, Montrose, Pennsylvania. 13" by 47". Designed by Sally Kallin, Pine Island Primitives.
"Sally's 'Mighty Oak' is a timeless design—one of my first rugs. I could hook it several more times in different colors and not tire of it."

Chilcott Leaves. Hooked by Martha Beals, Sidney, Maine. 81" by 37". Designed by Pearl K. McGown.

Antique Floral Bell Pull. Hooked by Lynda Hadlock, Manchester, New Hampshire. 40" by 7". Designed by Pearl K. McGown.

Newhall Scroll. Hooked by Anita Anderson, Groton, Massachusetts. 69" by 32". Designed by Pearl K. McGown.
"A tribute to my first teacher, Sally Newhall, who got me 'hooked.' My inspiration for color and scroll came from the Maine Waldoboro style. While this is not totally a 'scrap' rug, I had great fun hooking the leaves and small flowers from my scrap bag using four, five, and six cut."

Whimsical Leaves. Hooked by Marilyn L. Sly, Mystic, Connecticut. 44" by 29". Designed by Pearl K. McGown.
"For my first rug, I used inherited strips from Mother's many projects and her Pearl McGown pattern, 'Quickie.' While Mother would have crafted botanically correct leaves, she would be happy to see me developing my own hooking style. Background material dyed by Michele Micarelli."

Pine and Berries. Hooked by Lisa Larrabee, Rome, Maine. 72" by 32". Designed by Heirloom Rugs. "This is the second rug I started to hook in 2003. Martha Beals helped me to color plan and she dyed all the wool. 'Pine and Berries' is my hallway runner, and a 'bed' for my Pekingese dogs."

Sister Marion. Hooked by Nancy McCarthy, Newport Center, Vermont. 28" by 34". Designed by Sue Longchamps. "I purchased this design from The Rug Room, owned and operated by Sue Longchamps in East Burke, Vermont."

Rapture Small. Hooked by Diane Moore, Morgan, Vermont. 28" by 42". Designed by Jane McGown Flynn. "Florals are a favorite and I chose to concentrate on using dip-dyed fabrics to hook shaded flowers. The background was a spot-dyed yellow to create a light, happy, and warm feeling."

Nasturtiums. Hooked by Carol T. Dale, Gilford, New Hampshire. 28" by 45". Designed by Pearl K. McGown.
"I fell in love with the big nasturtiums and taught myself fine shading with this rug."

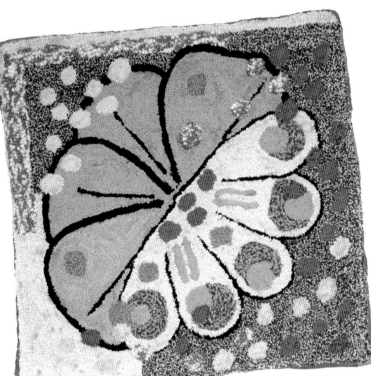

Spring Bloom. Designed and hooked by Ivana Vavakova, New York, New York. 27" by 27".
" 'Spring Bloom' is an exploration of texture, color, and fiber materials. My design was created on computer using Adobe Illustrator. The objective is to combine old technique and contemporary design."

Williams Antique. Hooked by Jan Hammond, Indianapolis, Indiana. 23" by 35". Designed by Kay Forbush for The House of Price, Inc.
"With the help of Pat Van Arsdale, the colors and modifications came into play. I love the colors."

Bless This House. Hooked by Janice E. Bogan, Clifton Park, New York. 25" by 40". Designed by McAdoo Rugs.
"This was a housewarming gift for my nephew Carlton, his wife Bolatito, and their children. McAdoo adapted the kit as I liked the border but wanted the center to reflect my heartfelt wish for a special blessing for their beautiful Maryland home. Thanks to Carlton and Bolatito for allowing me to borrow their rug for the show."

May Wildflowers. Designed and hooked by Marilyn L. Sly, Mystic, Connecticut. 17" by 17".
"My favorite spring wildflowers—mayflower, Dutchman's breeches, and dogtooth violets—adorn a mat for the rocking chair used by Grandmother, an ardent naturalist."

Poppy Field. Designed and hooked by Marcia Kent, Wilmington, Massachusetts. 22" by 20".
"Such a pleasure to hook a flower so brilliant and full of energy."

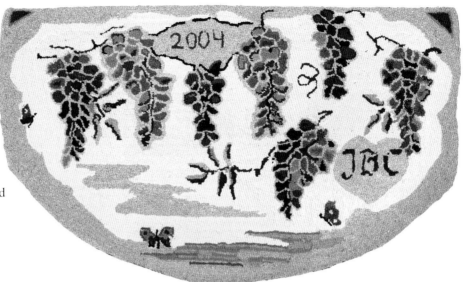

View From the Porch. Designed and hooked by Jane B. Clarke, Brattleboro, Vermont. 20" by 33".
"Saw a small wisteria stencil at Wal-Mart and the rug idea evolved from that. The overall design is mine. Signifies sitting on the porch looking out at a lawn, pond, butterflies, and overhead the wisteria. I started in 2004 and ended in 2006."

Sunflowers – Nicknamed Sunflowers for Leslie. Hooked by Terry Berntsen, Acworth, New Hampshire. 24" by 36". Designed by Susan Feller, Ruckman Mill Farm.
"I hooked this rug for my friend, Leslie Brennen, who loves sunflowers. It took me longer than planned since I couldn't work on it while she was there. Surprise! It was the first time I have used textures or plaids in my hooking."

Antique Dollhouse Rug. Hooked by Gail Majauckas, West Newbury, Massachusetts. 25" by 39". Designed by Underhill Farm.
"Design adapted from a tiny antique punch needle dollhouse rug."

Day Lily Impression. Designed and hooked by Peg Irish, Madbury, New Hampshire. 10" by 12".
"This piece was based on a photo of a special hybridized double white day lily in honor of my cousin, Margo Reed. The background uses a hand-painted dyed fabric."

Primitive Flowers. Designed and hooked by Mary Guay, Grand Isle, Vermont. 25" by 32".
"I wanted to design a primitive flower rug using three shade coloring."

Bert's Branch. Designed and hooked by Joanna Palmer, Melrose, Massachusetts. 16" by 21".
"Bertha is my eighty-five years young student who wanted a simple design to cover a footstool for her granddaughter."

Friendship. Hooked by Carol T. Dale, Gilford, New Hampshire. 26" by 41". Designed by Gardner King.
"This pattern from Mr. King's estate inspired me to hook in old-timey classic colors of red, green, antique black, and onion skin golds. The wools used and overdyed were from his estate as well."

Hydrangeas on Mohican Point. Designed and hooked by Carol Munson, Sunderland, Vermont. 22" by 27".
"The hydrangeas were planted roughly one hundred years ago on Mohican Point at Lake George, New York. The big white blooms announce the end of summer and time to leave this special family place."

Bird in Leaves. Hooked by Kathy Gage, South Burlington, Vermont. 20" by 28". Designed by Beverly Conway Designs.
"This rug is for my daughter-in-law, Kasara Gage."

Wildflowers of Northeast New England. Hooked by Marion B. Collins, South Burlington, Vermont. 40" by 27". Designed by Joan Moshimer. "Marion will be ninety-four on May 25th, 2006, and still going strong with rug hooking."

Wildflower Trellis. Hooked by Janis Ricker, New Castle, New Hampshire. 39" by 27". Designed by Joan Moshimer.

Bluebells. Hooked by Susan Gadapee, St. Johnsbury, Vermont. 24" by 35". Designed by Melinda Lapp, as featured by Red Clover Rugs.

80

Waldoboro Bird and Grapes.
Hooked by Janet Carruth,
Phoenix, Arizona. 15" by 16".
Designed by Jacqueline Hansen of
The 1840 House.
"Waldoboro is such a beautiful
style of rug hooking...it was such
fun to 'play with velvet' across the
surface of this piece."

Spring's Promise. Designed and hooked by Jo A. Weatherwax, Saratoga Springs,
New York. 25" by 39".
"Inspired by several rugs at the 2004 Green Mountain Rug Hooking Guild show.
Designed using seed catalogs as a guide for my first rug."

Mini Fantasy. Hooked by Ruth St. George, Shelburne, Vermont. 24" by 34". Designed by Yankee Peddler.

Mini Fantasy. Hooked by Geraldine North, Hanover, New Hampshire. 27" by 36". Designed by Yankee Peddler.
"I'm a gardener and this floral design caught my eye. I enjoyed designing the border."

Mini Fantasy. Hooked by Pamela Anfuso, Milford, New Hampshire. 34" by 25". Designed by Yankee Peddler.

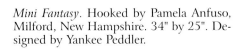

Museum Bed Rug. Hooked by Pamela Anfuso, Milford, New Hampshire. 50" by 40". Designed by Yankee Peddler.

Margaret's Garden. Hooked by Sherry M. Sollace, Alburg, Vermont. 36" by 36". Designed by Gwendolyn S. Gallup. "This rug is dedicated to my mother, Margaret M. Sollace, one of the strongest women I know. From my mother I learned how to make a house a home, make something from nothing, and be creative with my hands."

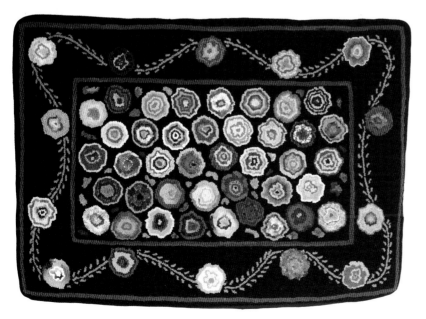

Favorite Flowers. Designed and hooked by Jeri Laskowski, Rochester, New York. 37" by 26".
"This is my interpretation of the familiar 'cat's paw' or 'mille fleur' designs. I decided to create a vine border to rest one's eyes on such a busy rug."

Olde Floral. Hooked by Sarah Guiliani, South Portland, Maine. 32" by 57". Designed by Woolley Fox LLC/Barb Carroll.
"This design is done with a #9 cut and it only took me five days to hook it. I love it!"

Flower Power. Hooked by Davey DeGraff, Hinesburg, Vermont. 28" by 42".
Designed by Vermont Folk Rugs.

Flower Box. Hooked by Donna Kenny, Lebanon, Connecticut. 50" by 38". Designed by Karen Kahle and Primitive Spirit.
"This is a Karen Kahle design that I took some artistic liberty with. Most of the buildings were changed to represent historical homes and churches surrounding the Lebanon Green in Lebanon, Connecticut."

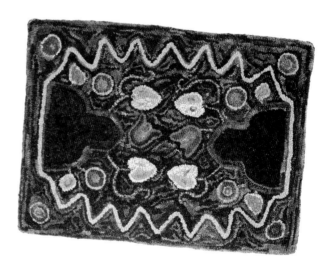

Tole Pattern. Hooked by Dot Harder, North Clarendon, Vermont. 20" by 32". Designed by Elizabeth Morgan.
"The inspiration for my rug was from a tole tray that Elizabeth Morgan gave to me for my birthday."

Country Farmhouse Floral. Designed and hooked by Sunnie Andress of Old Crow Farm, Newport, Vermont. 21" by 28".
"When creating this design, I pictured a country woman planning a 'serviceable' rug with brown and burgundy wools she'd saved. How happy she would be if a friend or relative brought a basket of colorful wool scraps so her rug could be beautiful as well as serviceable."

Blessings Heart. Hooked by "The Island Hookers," Lake Champlain Islands, Vermont, as a gift for Nancy Spier, Jericho, Vermont. Designed by Primitive Grace. Nancy Spier says, "This rug was designed by dear friend, DonnaSue Shaw. It was then hooked by six wonderful 'Island Hookers' as a housewarming gift for me. The initials of the ladies are located in each of the six leaves."

Variation on the Tree of Life. Hooked by Colleen Miller Hale, Grand Isle, Vermont. 23" by 37". Designer unknown, pattern found at a yard sale years ago. "I did this rug as my life was changing from a time of sadness to a time of joy. I didn't follow the shading I usually do, but rather used whirling reds and did the flowers whatever I felt like. I was becoming happy again."

Sweet Peas. Designed and hooked by Sandy Ducharme, Marshfield, Vermont. 36" by 27". "Flowers are one of Mother Nature's greatest gifts. My challenge was in creating the illusion of lush velvet roses. Capturing the lacy swaying effect for sweet peas was fun. I found my first attempt at hooking scrolls challenging. Background is leftover overdyed wool."

First Time Joy. Hooked by Karyn Lord, Plymouth, Massachusetts. 24" by 31". Designed by Patsy Becker.
"I think Patsy Becker is one of the most talented women in the world of rug hooking and it is always a pleasure to hook one of her designs. I love how my colors came together in 'First Time Joy' and the hit and miss border really makes my heart sing."

Penny Rug Sunflower. Hooked by Colleen Miller Hale, Grand Isle, Vermont. 17" by 28". Designed by Primitive Grace.
"My friend, DonnaSue, designed her first rug pattern collection. I chose to do the penny rug pattern. It was around Christmas that I started this rug, envisioning a holiday red and green rug. It started out red and green and then other colors showed up and created a bit of a stained glass effect."

Winter. Hooked by Barbara Pond, South Burlington, Vermont. 25" by 36". Designed by Harry M. Fraser Company.
"I hooked this rug pattern several years ago. It was a fun pattern and is the third one I've done. I gave it to my church bazaar to raffle in November. I borrowed it back from Pat McDonald, who won it."

Floral Garden. Hooked by Christine Detrick, Burlington, Vermont. 37" by 65". Designed by Margaret Mackenzie.

Paisley. Designed and hooked by Shirley Chaiken, Lebanon, New Hampshire. 15" by 15".
"Most of the original pattern for this Persian design was made of tiny leaves. It is now simplified, but the paisley shape still shows itself."

Anna's Candlelight. Hooked by Priscilla Buzzell, Newport, Vermont. 36" by 24". Designed by Louise Hunter Zeiser for Heirloom Rugs.
"A friend, Anna, had started this rug, but decided to give up hooking for health reasons. I was the lucky recipient and enjoyed making the rug."

Moss Rose. Hooked by Elizabeth M. Edwards, Williston, Vermont. 34" by 24". Designed by Karen Kahle and Primitive Spirit.

Penn Antique. Hooked by Tricia Travis, San Antonio, Texas. 44" by 35". Designed by Marion Ham – Quail Hill Designs.

Patience. Hooked by Janis Ricker, New Castle, New Hampshire. 38" by 26". Designed by Jane McGown Flynn.

Patience. Hooked by Joan Wheeler, Newport, Vermont. 39" by 25". Designed by Jane McGown Flynn. "Bought at The Dorr Mill Store many years ago when I first started hooking, but I never finished it until this year."

Metamorphosis. Hooked by Yvonne Isabelle, Williamstown, Vermont. 20" by 34". Designed by Jane McGown Flynn. "This is an old rug hooking teaching design in *Rug Hooking* magazine. I wanted to remember how to do the rose. The scroll was such a challenge—I did it my way!"

Metamorphosis. Hooked by Ruth Frost, East Montpelier, Vermont. 21" by 31". Designed by Jane McGown Flynn. "As an avid gardener I am fanatical about flowers. I would love to learn to shade as many as possible."

Floral. Hooked by Ruth Payne, Windsor, Vermont. 63" by 38". Designed by Charlotte Kimball Stratton.

"I began hooking this rug in 1957. When completed in 1960, my teacher, Mrs. Stratton, brought it to Detroit where it was displayed in Hudson's Department Store. When working on the rug I left a note for my husband one night, 'How do the pansies look?' He replied, 'Wilted.' "

Faithful (Modified). Hooked by Sandra E. Russell, Raymond, New Hampshire. 42" by 29". Designed by Mrs. Carl Hall.

"This pattern was a gift to me by one of my hooking friends from Peabody, Massachusetts. The flowers are mostly hand dyed wools with some purchased swatches. I love how the burgundy border sets off the old ivory interior and the hand dyed scrolls."

West of Eden. Hooked by Sandra E. Russell, Raymond, New Hampshire. 38" by 23". Designed by Harry M. Fraser Company.

"After hooking five floral rugs, I found this pattern with elephants, which are my husband Bob's favorite, and decided to hook it for him. I love seeing those elephants peeking out from behind the leaves. It has turned out to be one of my favorite rugs."

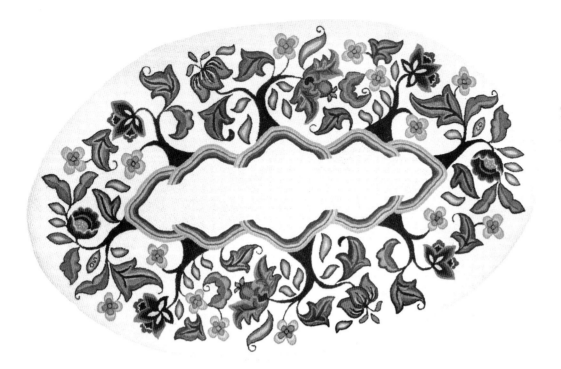

Queen Anne's Oval. Hooked by Susan Gadapee, St. Johnsbury, Vermont. 34" by 56". Designed by Joan Moshimer.

Floral Berry Classic Bed Rugg. Hooked by Margery Kimpton, Dunstable, Massachusetts. 72" by 48". Designed by George Kahnle for Hooked on the Creek.
"I found George Kahnle's 'Bed Rugg' at the April, 2004 Green Mountain Rug Hooking Guild show. Dick LaBarge helped me choose colors from his glorious stash to work in my blue toile bedroom. Back home I was thrilled when my classmate Eileen Friedrich was inspired to interpret George's design in her own color way." (Eileen's rug can be found on page 44.)

Oval Scroll. Hooked by Erika Egenes Anderson, Wesley Hills, New York. 28" by 43". Designed by Marion Ham – Quail Hill Designs.
"I have to give my friend Cecelia Toth credit for my hooking today. She introduced me to Marion Ham, who believes everyone can hook a rug. This is my second rug, which I started in Marion's workshop in North Carolina. I loved working on it."

Patrician #714. Hooked by Rebecca L. Cridler, Charles Town, West Virginia. 31" by 50". Designed by Pearl K. McGown.
"Always wanted a window like this. The pattern is not a stained glass design, but I saw it done by Pat Morgan in the McGown newsletter and fell in love with it."

Crazy Patch Primitive. Hooked by Beverly Delnicki, Wheelock, Vermont. 40" by 23". Designed by Jacqueline Hansen of The 1840 House.

Flowers and Squares. Hooked by Janet Hardy, Derby Line, Vermont. 40" by 30". Designed by Stephanie Krauss, Green Mountain Patterns.
"I like this pattern that Stephanie Krauss designed because it gave me the opportunity every week to create a new color scheme without having to plan ahead. The light and dark squares gave continuity while the patterns and colors gave diversity. I had great fun with this."

Jumbo Star. Hooked by Rebecca L. Cridler, Charles Town, West Virginia. 36" by 36". Designed by Lib Callaway. "First rug all from own dyeing of overdyed material."

The Lily. Hooked by Beverly Conway, Middlebury, Vermont. 52" by 52". Designed by Mary Simpson for Beverly Conway Designs.

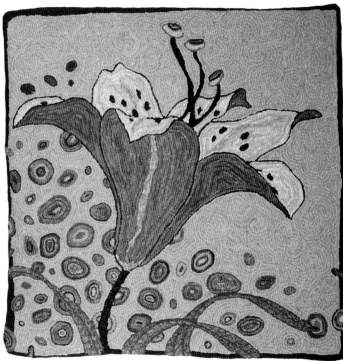

The Lily. Hooked by Arlene Jackman, Vergennes, Vermont. 49" by 49". Designed by Mary Simpson for Beverly Conway Designs. "I wanted something easy to do in the summer without thinking a lot about color. This was my choice and it was very easy."

Antique Flower Mat. Hooked by Carolyn Buttolph, St. Johnsbury, Vermont. 18" by 28". Designed by Cherylyn Brubaker, Hooked Treasures.
"I took the Hooked Treasures pattern, *Antique Flower Mat,* and added my own border. I liked Cherylyn Brubaker's execution of this rug. It's about texture and color."

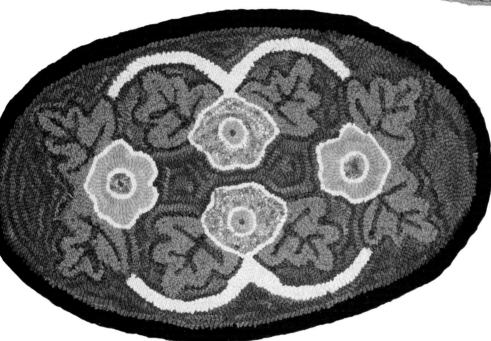

Floral. Hooked by Jane Ploof, Bristol, Vermont. 17" by 27". Designed by Yankee Peddler.
"This was my first rug. My wonderful sister-in-law, Susan Gingras, helped by giving me the pattern and wool for the background—and also encouragement. Other colors were purchased from Beverly Conway."

Yankee Sampler. Hooked by Susan Andreson, Costa Mesa, California. 9" by 23". Design adapted by Susan Andreson from a pattern by Joan Moshimer.
"This piece was inspired by old issues of *Rug Hooker news & views* and was adapted from a free pattern element designed by Joan Moshimer found in one of her magazines focusing on crewel designs."

Prelude. Hooked by Catherine Kane, South Egremont, Massachusetts. 20" by 24". Designed by Jane McGown Flynn.
"I started this at the Long Island Rug School with teacher Helen Connolly. It was Helen's rugs that inspired me to take up rug hooking. We color planned it together. Helen dyed the wool. My regular teacher, Liz Marino, taught me how to make the fringe from the rug's backing warp."

Mayflowers. Designed and hooked by Carolyn Buttolph of Red House Rugs, St. Johnsbury, Vermont. 27" by 15".
"My favorite, fragrant, early spring wildflowers inspired this rug."

Primitive Poppies. Hooked by Joan Wheeler, Newport, Vermont. 23" by 48". Designer unknown.
"I started this with Jeannie Benjamin at Green Mountain Rug School. I took out the pansies that were in it and put in padulas."

Peonies. Designed and hooked by Judy Quintman, Wilmington, North Carolina. 22" by 31".
"My inspiration came from the peonies blooming in our Vermont garden. I always loved seeing them and wanted to capture them in a rug."

Floral Fantasy. Designed and hooked by Cynthia Toolin, Enfield, Connecticut. 39" diameter.
"Adapted from a picture in a Dover copyright-free book. Punch needle."

Les Roses. Designed and hooked by Lucie Parrot, Roxboro, Quebec, Canada. 38" by 27".
"Roses are one of my favorite flowers. I wanted to mix flowers and geometrics. A lace curtain inspired me to join the flowers, the grid, and the ribbon."

Raven With Pumpkins. Designed and hooked by Maya Kearn, South Londonderry, Vermont. 46" by 64". "My very first rug. Inspired by the ravens in our yard and the roses and pumpkins in our garden. I designed and hooked this rug in September and October, 2005."

Roses #P627. Hooked by Sheila M. Breton, Surry, New Hampshire. 21" diameter. Designed by Jane McGown Flynn.

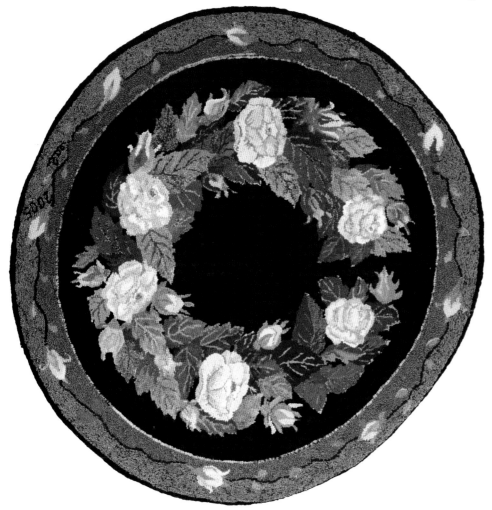

Circle of Roses. Hooked by Betty Bouchard, Richmond, Vermont. 38" diameter. Designer unknown.

Sue's Garden. Hooked by Susan Gadapee, St. Johnsbury, Vermont. 26" by 43". Designed by Susan Longchamps.

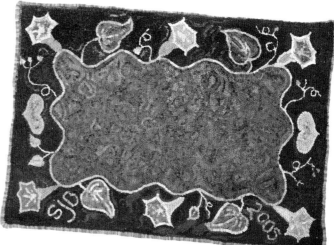

Morning Glory. Designed and hooked by Sara Burghoff, Underhill, Vermont. 25" by 36". "This rug reminds me of a wonderful reunion with my childhood friend Colette. I hadn't seen her since we were ten. I created this design for a rug camp in Virginia (my fiftieth birthday present) so that I could meet up with Colette. Sally Kallin was my terrific teacher."

Hammersmith Rug. Hooked by Shirley Chaiken, Lebanon, New Hampshire. 23" by 60". Designed by William Morris. "One of many rugs woven in the workshops at Kelmscott, Hammersmith, England c.1880; it is probably a late weaving of an earlier design."

99

Whig Rose. Hooked by Mary-Jean Janssen and Sue Janssen, Benson, Vermont. 14" diameter. Designed by Nancy Urbanak of Beaver Brook Crafts.

"This is my mom's one and only! Amy Oxford and Elizabeth Morgan helped her learn this summer—she was eighty-five. This chair pad exemplifies the marvelous versatility and adaptability of our craft as well as mom's enduring enthusiasm for learning. Mom passed away this winter so this holds many special memories."

Bridal Ring. Hooked by Susan Leskin, West Burke, Vermont. 35" by 63". Designed by Pearl K. McGown.

Chapter 7
The Twelve Days of Christmas

In 2005, Green Mountain Rug Hooking Guild member Susan Feller, from Augusta, West Virginia, coordinated a group project that celebrated and illustrated the well known holiday song, "The Twelve Days of Christmas." Thirteen different rug hookers took part in this joint effort. (Twelve people each hooked one of the twelve days, while a thirteenth hooked a runner with the title of the song.) Feller wrote a feature article in the November/December 2005 issue of *Rug Hooking* magazine about the project and the history of the song. She says, "The song is said to be a symbolic Catechism, or is it just a bawdy English tune 'enjoyed' by generations? The full article explores these directions. Each artist was interviewed about her experiences with the song and working on a collective project without seeing the others in progress."

The end results of this collaboration were on exhibit at this year's Shelburne show. The pieces put a new twist on an old favorite, including detachable drummers that can drum right off the rug and a cow that won't take any flack from milkmaids. And by the way, why hasn't anyone ever realized before that nine ladies dancing could be "Rockettes?"

Twelve Days of Christmas. Designed and hooked by Cynthia Norwood, Kirtland, Ohio. 14" by 51".
"I wanted to have feeling of antique and 'old English' holiday, thus used mainly paisleys from the 1800s and several fabrics of antique gold—all textured fabrics."

A Partridge in a Pear Tree. Designed and hooked by Anne Boissinot, Brampton, Ontario, Canada. 16" by 13".
" 'The Partridge' was the first of the twelve days of Christmas and it became a colorful entity that I embellished somewhat and made a bit funky for today's world."

Two Turtle Doves. Designed and hooked by Norma Batastini, Glen Ridge, New Jersey. 12" by 16".
"Creating this small mat combined two of my interests—rug hooking and bird watching. These colorful English doves were hooked with an assortment of leftover #3 and #4 cut strips. The background was hooked in a repetitious feather design imitating dense leaves on a tree or bush."

Three French Hens. Designed and hooked by Donna Hrkman, Dayton, Ohio. 12" by 16".
"I've always loved 'The Twelve Days of Christmas' and was thrilled to be invited to be in the challenge. I researched actual French chicken breeds and chose the prettiest and most distinctive ones. I wanted the design to be both whimsical and elegant."

Four Calling Birds. Designed and hooked by Kim Nixon, Maryville, Tennessee. 16" by 12".

Five Gold Rings. Designed and hooked by Fritz Mitnick, Pittsburgh, Pennsylvania. 12" by 16".

Six Geese-A-Laying. Designed and hooked by Katherine M. Porter, Chardon, Ohio. 12" by 16". "I love bold, graphic images and also circular motifs. There is no top or bottom. This pattern is non-directional so when it sits on a table it looks 'right' from any side."

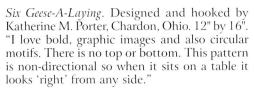

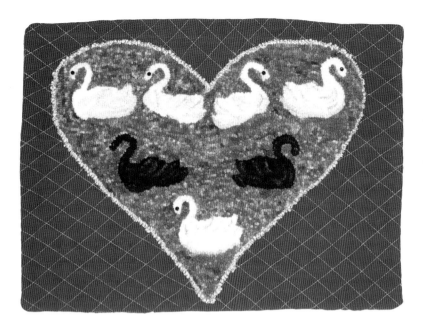

Seven Swans-A-Swimming. Designed and hooked by Betty A. Krull, Greer, South Carolina. 12" by 16".

"With a traditional approach to the words of the song, I chose the heart motif—a gift from 'my true love.' With inspiration from a friend's blue cameo, white and black swans 'swim' on the rich blue ground that is framed with a gold and ivory bezel and presented on red velvet."

Eight Maids-A-Milking. Designed and hooked by Nola A. Heidbreder, Saint Louis, Missouri. 12" by 16".

Nine Ladies Dancing. Designed and hooked by Rae Harrell, Hinesburg, Vermont. 17" by 12".
"My memory of seeing the 'Rockettes' at Radio City Music Hall in New York City inspired this design."

Ten Lords-A-Leaping. Designed and hooked by Beverly Conway, Middlebury, Vermont. 13" by 16".

Bringing Joy – Eleven Pipers Piping. Designed and hooked by Nancy D. Jewett, Pittsford, Vermont. 16" by 12".
"I was asked by *Rug Hooking* magazine to participate in a 'Twelve Days of Christmas' theme. Many ideas came to mind as characters for the pipers but nothing felt right until the idea of children being the pipers popped into my head. Drawing the children gave me great joy."

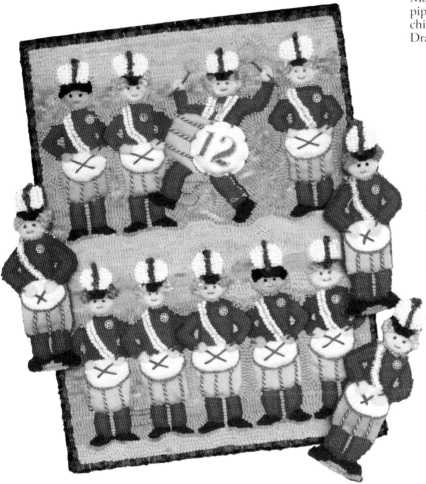

Twelve Drummers Drumming. Designed and hooked by Susanne McNally, Curtisville, Pennsylvania. 16" by 12".
"Asked to participate in a group effort—great fun. Always did like drum corps and marching bands."

Chapter 8
Children's Rugs

One of the Green Mountain Rug Hooking Guild's main missions is education.

Our members teach rug hooking classes to adults and children across the country, both to private individuals, in schools, and in many other settings. This year, the guild's education chairperson, Cheryl Connor, set up a special section of the show just for children, a little cozy room in the round barn called "The Kids' Hook Nook." School groups were invited and she singlehandedly taught sixty-five young people and several of their teachers how to hook rugs. The kids got to try traditional rug hooking as well as punch needle rug hooking. They were given a private tour of the show and most of them didn't want to leave their newfound craft. Their excitement about rug hooking was delightful and they added so much life to the exhibition. We look forward to expanding our children's program next year.

Horse With a Butterfly. Designed and hooked by Alexandra Sheldrick, age 11, Bridport, Vermont. 11" by 9".
"I drew the picture of a horse with a butterfly on its nose. I have hooked rugs for three years and I love hooking. I am eleven years old!"

Wild West. Designed and hooked by Grand Isle School's Kindergarten/1st Grade, with help from Melissa VanMarter-Rexford, Grand Isle, Vermont. 16" by 30".
"Inspired by their westward expansion unit, the Grand Isle School's Kindergarten/1st Grade class, taught by Sue Kolk, designed, color-planned, hooked, named, and finished this rug. I hooked with the children once a week for almost six months. Can you find the horns from the next ox-drawn wagon?"

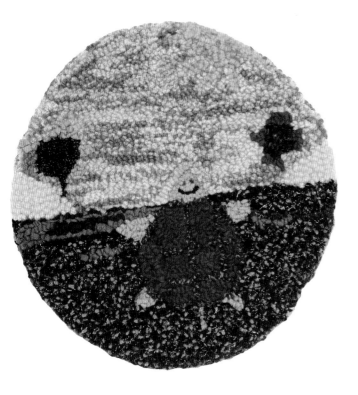

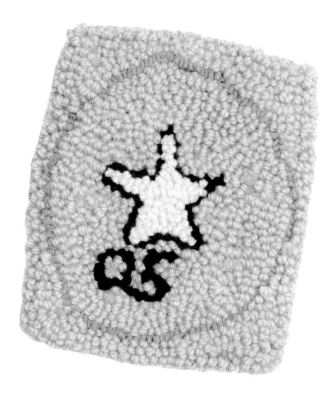

Turtle in the Sea. Hooked by Haven Tate and Susan Highley, Bridport, Vermont. 12" diameter. Designed by Haven Tate.
"I love turtles!" —Haven, age 8.
"This is Haven's first rug. We both did some of the hooking, both primitive and punch needle." —Susan (Haven's mom).

Red White and Blue Star. Designed and hooked by Hunter Carl, age 11, Bridport, Vermont. 8" by 7".
"I have taken rug hooking classes and learned how to do punch hooking. This year I tried to do traditional hooking and punch hooking in the same picture. Green is my favorite color."

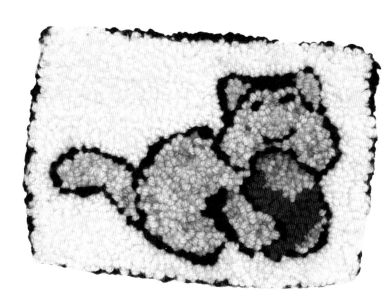

Teddy Bear and Heart Pillow. Hooked by Rachel Sheldrick, age 8, Bridport, Vermont. 9" by 8". Design adapted from copyright-free artwork found on the Internet.
"I have taken rug hooking classes for three years and decided to make a teddy bear pillow. I do punch hooking and I love to hook."

Kitten Rug. Hooked by Rachel Sheldrick, age 8, Bridport, Vermont. 7" by 10". Design adapted from copyright-free artwork found on the Internet.

Bunny Heart Pillow. Hooked by Meghan Santry, age 12, Middlebury, Vermont. 8" by 10". Designed by Karen Kahle and Primitive Spirit.

Be My Valentine. Designed and hooked by Mary Warren, High Bridge, New Jersey. 4" by 5".
"This heart is my first piece. My Junior Girl Scout Troop used the Green Mountain Rug Hooking Guild's education kits to learn to hook. It helped us earn the Sew Simple Badge."

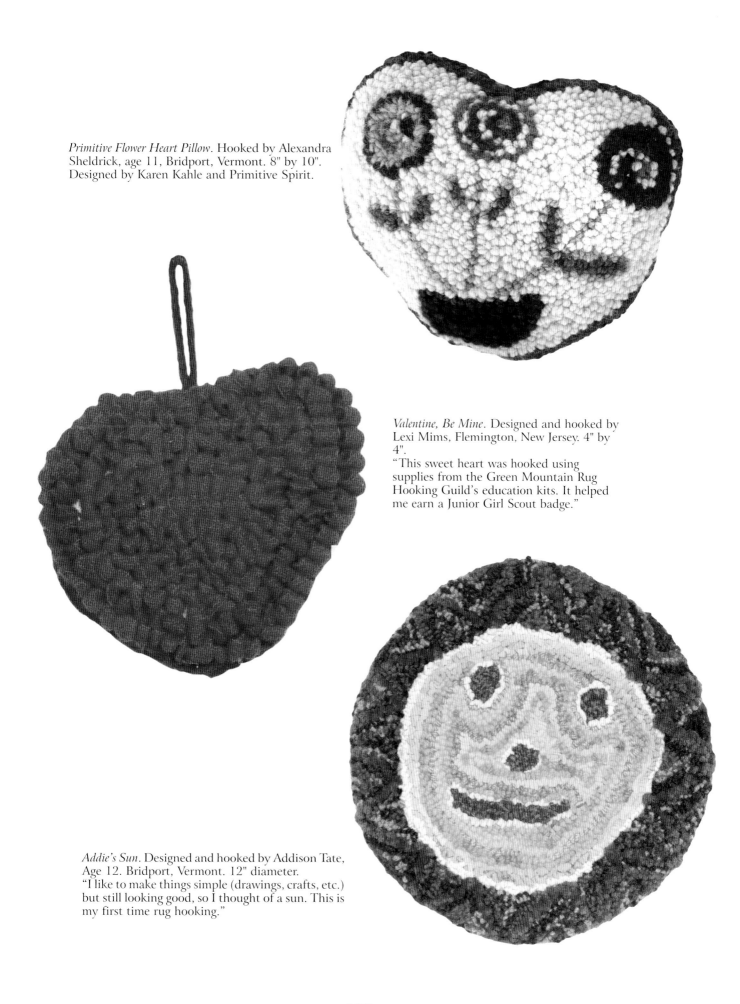

Primitive Flower Heart Pillow. Hooked by Alexandra Sheldrick, age 11, Bridport, Vermont. 8" by 10". Designed by Karen Kahle and Primitive Spirit.

Valentine, Be Mine. Designed and hooked by Lexi Mims, Flemington, New Jersey. 4" by 4".
"This sweet heart was hooked using supplies from the Green Mountain Rug Hooking Guild's education kits. It helped me earn a Junior Girl Scout badge."

Addie's Sun. Designed and hooked by Addison Tate, Age 12. Bridport, Vermont. 12" diameter.
"I like to make things simple (drawings, crafts, etc.) but still looking good, so I thought of a sun. This is my first time rug hooking."

109

Yellow Star Rug. Designed and hooked by Alexandra Sheldrick, age 11, Bridport, Vermont. 8" by 9".

Yellow Flower. Designed and hooked by Rachel Sheldrick, age 8, Bridport, Vermont. 12" by 8". "Yellow is my favorite color so I made a yellow flower. I usually punch hook but I will do traditional hooking this year."

Soccer Ball Geometric. Hooked by Hunter Carl, age 11, Bridport, Vermont. 8" by 8". Design adapted from copyright-free artwork found on the Internet.
"I made this design to look like a soccer ball."

110

Hot Air Balloon Pillow. Hooked by Steven Sickles, age 12, Addison, Vermont. 12" by 11". Design adapted from copyright-free artwork found on the Internet.

Yellow Tulip. Hooked by Steven Sickles, age 12. Addison, Vermont. 9" by 7". Design adapted from copyright-free artwork found on the Internet. "This rug is punched and traditionally hooked. This is my first try at traditional hooking."

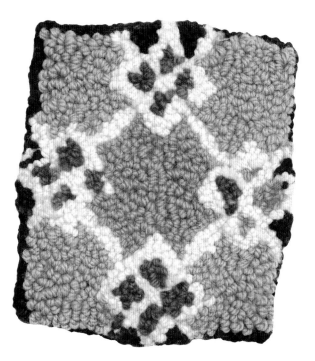

Geometric Pillow. Hooked by Hunter Carl, age 11, Bridport, Vermont. 8" by 10". Design adapted from copyright-free artwork found on the Internet.
"I liked this pattern because it reminded me of a baseball diamond."

Geometric Rug. Hooked by Steven Sickles, age 12, Addison, Vermont. 7" by 8". Design adapted from copyright-free artwork found on the Internet.

Children's Art Immortalized By Grown Ups

The following five hooked pieces were all made by parents who used their young children's artwork for their patterns. What a wonderful way to immortalize a favorite drawing or painting! Capturing that little child's imaginative world in hundreds, if not thousands of small hooked loops sends the message that they are loved and that their creativity is treasured, encouraged, and appreciated. It also helps us to remember their more innocent moments when they get old enough to start asking us for the car keys!

My Cat Oreo. Hooked by Lisa Mims, Flemington, New Jersey. 10" by 10". Designed by Lexi Mims.
"I love to hook my daughter Lexi's drawings! Marianne Lincoln taught me the reverse hooking technique used in my background. It makes me happy to look at this piece."

Melissa's Fairy. Designed and hooked by Kathleen Menzies, Greenfield Park, Quebec, Canada. 35" by 20".
"My daughter Melissa drew this playful fairy when she was five. I felt that this being would make a wonderful rug and adapted the drawing for the purpose."

Best Friends. Hooked by LeeAnn Metropoulos, Lebanon, New Jersey. 29" by 34". Designed by Olivia Metropoulos.
"My daughter, Olivia, drew this picture when she was four. It is a picture of her with her two best friends, Sammy and Katey. Of course, Olivia is the one with the fancy hair."

Gobble, Gobble. Designed and hooked by Laurie Lausen, Minneapolis, Minnesota. 11" by 18".
"One of my favorite antique rugs is a simple mat with two roosters facing each other. My rendition uses my son's preschool artwork...the priceless 'turkey hand print' to create this treasured family heirloom."

Sahale's Santa. Hooked by Claudia Casebolt, Lawrenceville, New Jersey. 19" by 41". Designed by Sahale Casebolt.
"My daughter, Sahale, drew this Santa, reindeer, and stars on a 'toilet paper roll' shaped Christmas ornament when she was about seven years old. I unrolled it, blew the image up, and hooked it. Note the Jewish stars with the Santa—truly nondenominational."

Chapter 9
Architectural

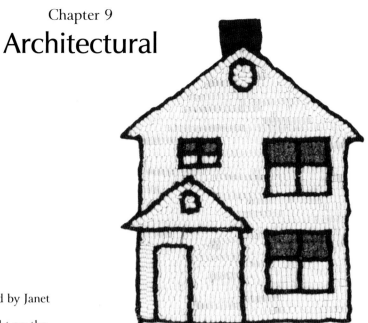

Chebeague Island House. Designed and hooked by Janet Conner, Hiram, Maine. 25" by 29".
"I designed and hooked this piece sitting right on the porch of this very house during rug camp! The Chebeague Island House is where strong women go to get stronger."

Saltbox Row. Hooked by Anne "Tina" Fisler, Jericho, Vermont. 16" by 29". Designed by Wendy Miller.
"This is my first rug, and I am grateful to my wonderful Richmond, Vermont rug hooking group for all their help—as well as to Patsy Becker, my first rug school teacher, who added my two cats to the original Wendy Miller design."

Townhome Sweet Townhome. Hooked by Claudia Casebolt, Lawrenceville, New Jersey. 24" by 28". Design adapted by Claudia Casebolt from an antique rug.
"The rug is an adaptation of an antique rug with my house substituted for the house on the original rug. We live at a boarding school, in a townhouse on campus identical to the townhouses of twenty other teachers. I like to think that inside it's unique."

Oak Bluffs. Hooked by Amy Spokes, South Burlington, Vermont. 23" by 44". Designed by Stephanie Krauss with suggestions by Amy Spokes.
"As a little girl, I used to visit my grandparents in their gingerbread house in Oak Bluffs. The old white houses are now multicolored. These are not replicas of any, just my imagination."

115

Paris Street. Designed and hooked by Gwenn C. Smith, Lebanon, New Hampshire. 12" by 24". "Paris! I love it! I took many pictures when I was there last year. This is a typical scene—little shops, cafés, alleys, all with the unmistakable charm that is Paris."

Café at Jardin Du Luxembourg. Designed and hooked by Gwenn C. Smith, Lebanon, New Hampshire. 19" by 26". "This little café in the Jardin du Luxembourg in Paris is one of my favorites. The park is full of families on weekends and the café has many more outside tables than depicted here. The park, the children, the lovers, the sounds of Parisians chattering. One of the charming sights of Paris."

116

The House of Golden Stars. Designed and hooked by Virginia Gregg, Falmouth, Massachusetts. 25" by 36".
"My son David bought this house in Providence, Rhode Island when still a bachelor. I was reminded of these words in a song he had made up when just a child and wondered who he would find to share his house. He is married now and that is my grandson, Sam, watching for my arrival every Thursday."

Entertainment by Jona. Clap. Hooked by Sarah Madison, Amherst, Massachusetts. 33" by 22". Designer unknown.
"Inspired by a c.1740s tavern sign in Easthampton, Massachusetts."

Advent. Designed and hooked by Jean W. Beard, Hanover, New Hampshire. 16" by 11".
"During the season of Advent I arrange for wreaths with purple bows to be placed on the doors of my church. I was baptized at four months of age, on the third Sunday in Advent, so I give the wreaths in memory of my parents."

Attorney Trade Sign – G. M. D. Bloss. Hooked by Karl Gimber, Carversville, Pennsylvania. 23" by 26". Designed by Mary Jo Gimber. "Inspired by antique trade sign and Mary Jo's ancestor, an attorney in Ohio, 1823."

Blue Ball Inn Tavern Sign. Hooked by Karl Gimber, Carversville, Pennsylvania. 25" by 21". "Inspired by an antique tavern sign in York Heritage Trust, York, Pennsylvania."

Peace on Earth Tavern Sign. Hooked by Gwen Kjelleren, South Hero, Vermont. 46" by 26". Designed by Primitive Grace. "This rug is from the first collection of hooked rug patterns by Primitive Grace. This design has a wonderfully appealing folk art quality and charm, and combines my love of lions, old trade signs, and motto rugs. Thanks so much to my dear and truly talented friend, DonnaSue Moquin Shaw!"

118

Morris' Fleur-De-Lys (2004).
Hooked by Jocelyn Guindon,
Montreal, Quebec, Canada. 29" by
23". Design adapted by Jocelyn
Guindon from the artwork of
William Morris.

Stained Glass Treasures – One. Hooked by Beth
McDermet, Marlboro, Vermont. 24" by 22". Design
adapted by Beth McDermet from antique stained glass.

Stained Glass Treasures – Two. Hooked by Beth
McDermet, Marlboro, Vermont. 24" by 22". Design
adapted by Beth McDermet from antique stained glass.
"These rugs are copied from a pair of 1920s stained
glass windows, given to us by my sister for our
Victorian home in Salem, Massachusetts. When we
moved to Vermont last year, we decided to leave the
windows with the house, but their memory lives on in
the rugs."

Many Moons. Designed and hooked by Molly W. Dye, Jacksonville, Vermont. 22" by 33".
"March of 2005 we had brilliant starry nights with voluminous clouds racing to get somewhere. I would wake and watch the night show and wonder about a dying friend who would soon depart from the Vermont landscape. We were asked to plant seedlings in her memory so I sowed many moonflowers."

Mimi's House. Hooked by LeeAnn Metropoulos, Lebanon, New Jersey. 23" by 35". Designed by Emily Robertson.
"My grandmother, Mimi, moved into this house when she was one. She grew up here along with her older sister and twin brother. She stayed in the house after she married my grandfather Baba, and they raised my mother here. My grandmother just turned ninety-two and she still lives here."

Ottawa Tulips. Designed and hooked by Barbara Lukas, Ottawa, Ontario, Canada. 11" by 15".
"Ottawa's annual Tulip Festival and Parliament Buildings."

Well Combed Home. Designed and hooked by Linda Helms, Jeffersonville, Vermont. 23" by 36".
"This is my best friend's home. It perfectly suits her. She is turning twenty-nine again and I wanted to do something special for her from far away. So, Happy Birthday ReeRee. Love, Pee Wee."

Carney Hollow. Designed and hooked by Sharon Lesio, Springwater, New York. 26" by 36".
"I started this rug in Emily Robertson's 2005 class at Shelburne. My husband and I had just purchased this new home. I drew the rug the way I wanted the house to look when it was finished, and the snow had melted. I couldn't forget our dogs, Bella and Katie."

Churches For All Seasons. Hooked by Stephanie Gibson, St. Clairsville, Ohio. 30" by 30". Designed by Stephanie Gibson and Tonya Benson. "Inspired by 'Inspirations from the Heart and Soul' by Tonya Benson (Mad Hen Primitives, Marietta, Ohio.) Her drawings are unique and fun to incorporate into a rug. Love it."

Nathan Plympton House. Designed and hooked by Kim Dubay, North Yarmouth, Maine. 24" by 30".
"I wanted to commemorate my home in a rug as it celebrates becoming 200 years old. The house was named for Nathan Plympton as the first postmaster of North Yarmouth, Maine, which is also the location of my rug hooking studio, Primitive Pastimes."

Quaker Bridge Road. Designed and hooked by Peggie Cunningham, Hightstown, New Jersey. 29" by 33".
"This is my childhood home and my earliest recollections: cats, fields of flowers, an old apple tree, and a lovely weeping cherry tree."

Frank Lynam's Cabin. Designed and hooked by Tracy Jamar, New York, New York. 18" by 23".
"This log cabin was built about 1898 in northwestern Wisconsin by my grandfather, Frank Lynam. As a child, I spent every summer there with my family. I cherish my two weeks there every September still. Frank Lynam was born April 14, 1866 and died October 8, 1950."

Blacky. Hooked by Donna Y. Brandt, Flemington, New Jersey. 21" by 23". Designed by Andrew Yosua.
"In honor of my father's 70th birthday, I hooked a picture, drawn by my brother, of a cabin in Black Moshannon State Park. My family has vacationed there since I was a baby. Now PopPop and Grandma share the fun with their grandchildren too!"

Combstead. Designed and hooked by Joyce Combs, Lambertville, New Jersey. 26" by 35".
"This will always be 'the home of my heart' because my husband and I raised our sons here."

Grandpa's Woodshed. Hooked by Yvonne Isabelle, Williamstown, Vermont. 22" by 31". Design adapted by Yvonne Isabelle from the artwork of Eric Sloane.
"I started this rug with Emmy Robertson in June 2005 at rug school and chose the woodshed because I love barns. I made it with the feel of spring. The woodshed is empty! Enjoyed hooking the shed and large stone wall."

Don't Sit Under the Apple Tree with Anyone Else But Me. Hooked by Lisa Mims, Flemington, New Jersey. 24" by 35". Designed by Lisa Mims, with drawing help and guidance from Emily Robertson and Trish Becker. "Hooked with much love for my dad, Richard Lamperti, for his 70th birthday. This dear home was built by his parents, Charles and Virginia. They were married in it and lived there for almost fifty years. It proudly sits at 88 Norwood Avenue, North Plainfield, New Jersey."

Chapter 10

Animals

When all of the rugs arrived for the show they were sorted into groups to help make the hanging of the show run more smoothly. With the help of hand scrawled signs for guidance, volunteers carried the rugs to their proper piles. The florals were put here, the "Strong Women" there. Rugs were thigh-high and knee-deep everywhere you looked. (It was wonderful.) If you wanted to find the animal rugs, however, you didn't have to read the signs, you just had to look for the most enormous pile. Yes, members of the Green Mountain Rug Hooking Guild have great affection for their animals. Whether faithful family pets, charming barnyard residents, or wild animals never met in person, these creatures are brought to life on rugs with great care and lots of personality.

The animals shown here include cats, birds, sheep, cows, and wild animals. All other animals, including dogs, horses, chickens, roosters, rabbits, insects, donkeys, monkeys, reptiles, fish, and many other assorted beasts, are featured in this book's companion volume.

Cats

Kitty Cat. Hooked by Susan Gingras, Weybridge, Vermont. 19" by 19". Design adapted from the folk art of M Shaw by Kris Miller and Spruce Ridge Studios.
"I love to hook cats! This one was irresistible!"

My Kitty Beast. Designed and hooked by Jean Brinegar, Mt. Holly, Vermont. 20" by 30". "The great McKeester was in my life for a short time, so I hooked this rug in her memory. She was so full of life and always in trouble."

Catfish. Hooked by Karen Maddi-Perks, Chicago, Illinois. 28" by 62". Design adapted from the folk art of M Shaw by Kris Miller and Spruce Ridge Studios.
"When I first saw this pattern, I knew I had to hook the tail in brilliant blues and greens. Initially I hooked a conventional brown striped tabby cat, but a midnight epiphany at camp drew me to an aqua overdyed texture that made perfect stripes, integrating the body with the fishtail."

Posy Rug. Hooked by Robin H. Falta, Cornwall, Vermont. 26" by 38". Designed by Patsy Becker.
"This is one of the first rugs I have hooked with all wool that I dyed myself, and I love it—both dyeing wool and the rug."

Fish Bones. Designed and hooked by Leslie Goldring, Ferrisburg, Vermont. 19" by 18".
"I wanted to hook a cat with distinctly triangular shaped tiger stripes. The fish skeleton on a plate just wanted to be in on the fun."

Great Cat. Hooked by Judith Latour, Granby, Massachusetts. 22" by 32". Designed by Woolley Fox LLC/Barb Carroll.

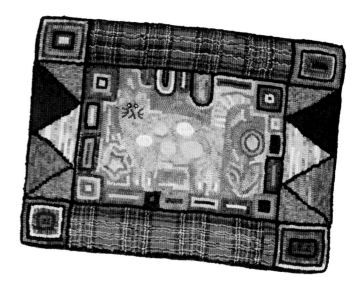

Marmalade. Hooked by Kathleen Menzies, Greenfield Park, Quebec, Canada. 20" by 27". Designed by Loretta Bluher-Moore with borders designed and added by Kathleen Menzies.

Country Cat. Hooked by Suzanne Jern, Wallingford, Vermont. 26" by 31". Designed by Claire Murray. "Being a cat lover, I just couldn't resist this cat."

Matty. Designed and hooked by Elizabeth Guth, Tunbridge, Vermont. 31" by 45".
"This rug was a surprise present. It was designed from a photo of a beloved cat sitting on a table, with a vase of flowers in front of a painting, with colors that were desired. The name of the cat and folk art birds needed to be included also."

What's Ya Doing? Designed and hooked by Karen Balon, Goffstown, New Hampshire. 18" by 18".
"Orion, one of my four cats. The curious one. Always wondering what you're doing. Always wanting to take part in what is going on. I just had to capture him this way, so when I look at this piece it will always bring a smile to my heart."

Perseus. Designed and hooked by Karen Balon, Goffstown, New Hampshire. 18" by 18".
"Out of four cats, this is my serious one. When I think of Perseus, this is how I always picture him and how I will always remember him, even after he's gone."

Guard Cat. Hooked by Sandi Goldring, Essex Junction, Vermont. 27" by 38". Designer unknown.

Theo Cat. Hooked by Jeni Nunnally, Cape Neddick, Maine. 29" by 37". Designed by Marion Ham – Quail Hill Designs.
"I loved this rug design by Marion Ham and made it my own by adding my husband Bob's name and the name and coloring of 'his' cat, who is part Bengal."

Heppy. Hooked by Sandi Goldring, Essex Junction, Vermont. 27" by 32". Designed by Patsy Becker.

Hildy. Hooked by Sandi Goldring, Essex Junction, Vermont. 29" by 47". Cat drawn by Rae Harrell on log cabin pattern. "Being a recycler at heart, this rug started out to be utilitarian with the three colors that were most abundant in my clothes pile. When it started to look dreary, Rae Harrell agreed to draw our cat, Hildy, lying on the unfinished section."

Cat Family. Hooked by Nell Berntsen, Acworth, New Hampshire. 18" by 34". Designed by DiFranza Designs. "One of my coworkers and I decided to do this series of rugs. It's a lot of fun to see how our color choices look and how our hooking techniques differ."

Smokie – Fat Cat. Hooked by Joanne Miller, Canaan, New Hampshire. 29" by 27". Designed by Patsy Becker. "Patsy Becker's 'Fat Cat' is such a perfect resemblance of our son and daughter-in-law's pet Smokie, I couldn't resist hooking it for them."

128

Oriental Rug Cats. Hooked by Nell Berntsen, Acworth, New Hampshire. 18" by 34". Designed by DiFranza Designs. "The inspiration was a piece of spot-dyed fabric by Stephanie Krauss. When I saw it, I knew exactly what I would do with it. It reminded me of some chintz patterns on some English china."

Ruskin Cat. Hooked by Jeni Nunnally, Cape Neddick, Maine. 37" by 24". Designed by Charles Francis Annesley Voysey. "A woodblock print adapted from a design by English architect and designer, C.F.A. Voysey (1857-1941). This was my second rug."

Cats and Rose Vines. Hooked by Karyn Lord, Plymouth, Massachusetts. 20" by 44". Designed by Barbara Brown, Port Primitives. "Barbara Brown adapted this pattern from an antique rug hooked in the late 1800s. I fell in love with this design the moment I saw it, perhaps because I am so fond of cats. I used soft, muted colors in an attempt to make my rug look old too."

Cats and Pineapple. Hooked by Jane Ploof, Bristol, Vermont. 21" by 44". Designed by Beverly Conway Designs. "I love cats, and with the pineapple as a sign of welcome, I thought it an appropriate rug to welcome two new cats to our house. Beverly Conway and Susan Gingras were very helpful with color choices."

Meow. Designed and hooked by Joelle Hochman, Somerville, Massachusetts. 14" by 15".
"Third in a series of animal mats inspired by my daughter's love of anything furry."

Lib in Sunshine. Designed and hooked by Shelley Poremski, Florence, Vermont. 13" by 16".
"My eighteen-year-old cat, Lib, spends most of the summer lying on our stone wall, basking in the sun. I punch hooked this wall hanging of him as a Christmas gift for my daughter, Hilary."

Monkey. Designed and hooked by Jean W. Beard, Hanover, New Hampshire. 19" by 26".
"I offered to take care of a friend's cat in my apartment for two weeks, and ended up having him for three months. Needless to say, I became very attached to Monkey."

Friends. Designed and hooked by Sally W. Kirouac, Saratoga Springs, New York. 30" by 24".
"Real life is fantastical. We've actually seen our cat, Willow, drinking from our birdbath with a very reckless bird waiting his turn on the rim."

My Favorite Spot. Designed and hooked by Judy Dodds, Waitsfield, Vermont. 25" by 16".
"This piece grew out of a dye class with Peg Irish in which I painted on the fabric, then cut and hooked it in consecutive strips to form a landscape for the background. Kitsa found his way into the design next to the window on an antique crazy quilt."

Birds, Ducks, Geese, and Other Things With Wings

Untitled. Hooked by Joanna Palmer, Melrose, Massachusetts. 40" by 25". Designed by George Palmer. "Native Northeast Indian inspirations."

Waldoboro Birds. Hooked by Cecelia K. Toth, New York, New York. 22" by 32". Designed by Jacqueline Hansen of The 1840 House.
"Inspired by a traditional Waldoboro method design."

Birds & Pomegranates. Hooked by Linda Jackson, Newbury, Massachusetts. 22" by 40". Designed by Edyth C. O'Neill.
"My first rug—finally completed with valuable input and encouragement from my fabulous and talented hooker friends. Thank you one and all!"

Birds & Pomegranates. Hooked by Helen Johnson, Brookfield, Vermont. 25" by 43". Designed by Edyth C. O'Neill.
"I love this rug because of the large motifs, but didn't want to do it in traditional colors. I'm the kid who had to use all the colors in the crayon box. Pattern was also adapted by changing the leaves and vase."

George (St. John from "Book of Kells"). Hooked by Helen Wolfel, Barre, Vermont. 24" by 19". Design adapted by Helen Wolfel from *Book of Kells.*
"I took a class with Doris Norman in Truro, Nova Scotia. I wanted to do something a little different and St. John reminded me of my husband, George."

Indigo Bunting. Designed and hooked by Ian A. Hodgdon, Montpelier, Vermont. 12" by 18".
"While visiting Stephanie Krauss, I noticed a photograph a patron had sent her of an indigo bunting. I asked if I could use it for a pattern, and in short order I was dyeing wool and hooking away."

Schwenkfelder Bird. Hooked by Mary Jo Gimber, Carversville, Pennsylvania. 14" by 19". Design adapted from a fraktur by Mary Jo Gimber.
"The inspiration for the design was a Pennsylvania German fraktur drawing. It was raffled to benefit the Schwenkfelder Library and Heritage Center and Hunterdon County Rug Artisans Guild in September 2006."

Funky Bird. Designed and hooked by Peggie Cunningham, Hightstown, New Jersey. 10" by 16".
"A mixed media workshop with Gail Dufresne prompted me to create this funky bird for my granddaughter."

Anything Goes. Hooked by Edith McClure, Farmington, Connecticut. 29" by 39". Designed by Pris Buttler Rug Designs.
"This peacock has been wonderfully fun to create. Inspired by Abby Vakay, I started experimenting with new techniques and adding unusual materials including beads and mirrors."

Fraktur Goose. Designed and hooked by Diane Gage, Akron, Pennsylvania. 20" by 20".
"The design for this rug is an adaptation of a goose design I found in a corner of a fraktur when I was visiting a Lancaster County, Pennsylvania historical museum."

The Gift. Hooked by Dorothy Panaceck, Fredericksburg, Texas. 26" by 32". Designed by Jule Marie Smith.
"Jule designed this rug in a class at the Star of Texas Rug Camp. She gave each of us in the class a paper pattern. She added Texas Bluebonnets for a Texas flair. I was in Barb Carroll's class later and the crow became red. It was truly a gift."

Waldoboro Parrot. Hooked by Jeni Nunnally, Cape Neddick, Maine. 20" by 29". Designed by Jacqueline Hansen of The 1840 House.
"Since Jackye was my first teacher and she is the 'Queen of Waldoboro,' it seemed a no-brainer that my first rug be a Waldoboro. It was fun to do!"

Paint Pot Puffin. Hooked by Jane Clarke, Brattleboro, Vermont. 17" by 16". Designer unknown.
"Picked this burlap design up at a library in Amherst. It was a dirty old design on a table selling old secondhand items. I used the colors I wanted and not the usual (for better or worse). Made it to fit a Boston rocker."

Cardinal in Holly. Hooked by Anne "Tina" Fisler, Jericho, Vermont. 14" diameter. Designed by Nancy Urbanak of Beaver Brook Crafts.
"I'm pretty sure this Nancy Urbanak design was intended as a chair seat, but I put it right on my table instead—because a cardinal is too pretty to sit on!"

Crow With Berries. Hooked by Theresa Boise, Middlebury, Vermont. 17" by 21". Designed by Jeanne Benjamin.
"I see many crows and other birds feasting on the berries from my crab apple tree so I knew I had to hook this design."

Osprey With Kokanee. Designed and hooked by Sara Judith, Nelson, British Colombia, Canada. 44" by 31".
"The osprey, or fish hawk, is a strong bird catching fish in its powerful talons. Our area, the Kootenays, has the second largest concentration of these birds in the world. In the fall they feed on Kokanee, a species of landlocked salmon that turn red when they spawn."

Bird's Lunch. Hooked by Dawn McConnell, Middlesex, Vermont. 11" by 13". Designed by Susan Feller, Ruckman Mill Farm.
"Hooked in the Waldoboro style. Hand dyed wool by Stephanie Krauss."

Going Home. Designed and hooked by Emma Webber, Petaluma, California. 24" by 20.
"I think there's a cluster of three birds and a single. The background is typical of a series I did. I wouldn't want a realistic sky."

Midnight Rendezvous. Hooked by Jeni Nunnally, Cape Neddick, Maine. 30" by 29". Designed by Yoshiko Yamamoto.
"A woodblock design by Yoshiko Yamamoto of Arts and Crafts Press Designs."

Forever Friends. Designed and hooked by Laurie Lausen, Minneapolis, Minnesota. 20" by 31".
"A celebration of friendship! Hooking this rug was a personal journey…a meditation on relationships, transitions, and the relocation of a dear friend."

Apple and Pear Trees. Hooked by Brenda Williams, Valatie, New York. 36" by 53". Designed by George Kahnle for Hooked on the Creek.

Startled. Designed and hooked by Ruth McLoughlin, Rochester, Vermont. 26" by 32".
"There is a pond nearby where the Canada geese stop over before heading south. This rug tries to capture them."

Berry Pickers. Hooked by Janet C. Berner, South Newfane, Vermont. 15" by 28". Designed by Yankee Peddler.

Dawdling Ducks. Designed and hooked by Susan DeGregorio, Salem, New Hampshire. 11" by 15".
"A whimsical rug mat for a stool. I used a simple design so I could 'play' with the colors and textures of the wool."

Great Horned Owl. Designed and hooked by Ruth McLoughlin, Rochester, Vermont. 24" by 21".
"The idea for this rug came after surprising a very large and vocal owl on a canoe trip. It made me want to learn more about their lives and habitat."

Snowy Owl. Hooked by Helen Wolfel, Barre, Vermont. 22" by 17". Designed by Jane McGown Flynn.
"Luise Wolfel, my mother-in-law, hooked this pattern in the late 1960s to early 1970s. She sold it to someone but then they never paid her for it. I always felt bad about this and wanted to have the picture in our home, so I made one of my own."

In Flight. Hooked by Jane Ploof, Bristol, Vermont. 19" by 45". Designed by Beverly Conway Designs.
"I had seen this pattern and fell in love with it. The sunflowers had to be bright and cheerful. I had some great input for color selections from Susan Gingras and Beverly Conway. This rug makes me feel like spring."

In Flight. Hooked by Karen Maddi-Perks, Chicago, Illinois. 20" by 44". Designed by Beverly Conway Designs.
"Begun in Beverly's class. I was inspired by her richly colored overdyed textures, and used many in the flowers and sky. I also particularly enjoyed using many solid dark colors of similar value that, taken together, read as 'black' for the crows."

Mirror Image. Hooked by Geraldine North, Hanover, New Hampshire. 21" by 39". Design adapted by Geraldine North from a friend's antique rug.
"My friend's rug was badly worn but the ducks were wonderful. I had to hook those ducks and keep them afloat."

Fine Feathered Friends. Designed and hooked by Roberta Smith, West Windsor, New Jersey. 26" by 40".
"I enjoy bird watching and decided to hook a few favorites to have in the house."

Winter Feeding. Designed and hooked by Ruth McLoughlin, Rochester, Vermont. 26" by 32".
"Watching the birds at our deck feeder inspired this design."

Almond Blossoms. Hooked by Linda Jackson, Newbury, Massachusetts. 15" by 19". Designed by Karen Kahle and Primitive Spirit.

Almond Blossoms. Hooked by Judith Latour, Granby, Massachusetts. 15" by 19". Designed by Karen Kahle and Primitive Spirit.

Almond Blossoms. Hooked by Suzanne Dirmaier, Waterbury Center, Vermont. 15" by 17". Designed by Karen Kahle and Primitive Spirit.
"I wanted to do a rug for my niece's first child. Perusing through Karen Kahle's catalog, I found the description of this design. Its inspiration was Van Gogh's 'Almond Blossoms,' which he painted for his new nephew. Perfect for my new great-nephew."

Tweedy Birds. Designed and hooked by Kathie Barbour, Hanover, New Hampshire. 33" by 55".
"This design is an adaptation of an Egyptian folk art appliqué wall hanging. The birds are hooked with tweeds and other textured as-is wools from my stash of thrift shop skirts, shirts, and jackets."

Sheep

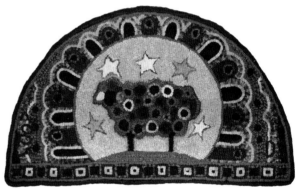

Wooley Girls Wow. Hooked by Mary Pringle, South Hero, Vermont. 20" by 36". Designed by Primitive Grace.
"We have sheep at our farmhouse and I was pleased to hook this rug from the first collection of my friend DonnaSue's new venture, Primitive Grace hooked rug patterns."

Wooly Girl Wow. Hooked by DonnaSue Shaw, Grand Isle, Vermont. 17" by 29". Designed by Primitive Grace.
"I had so much fun pulling strips from my scrap basket to hook this rug. When I was finished, I noticed I mistook dark green for black in a few spots. I just can't watch football and hook at the same time!"

Curly in Vine. Designed and hooked by Sherry Kelley, Rutland, Vermont. 22" by 30".
"This is my first traditional hooked rug. I've been a puncher for sixteen years. The drawing happened when I had these colors to cut in strips and had to make a design that would incorporate them. I wasn't sure if traditional hooking would be for me. Now I love it!"

Ann's Corriedale. Hooked by Gail Mueller, Orillia, Ontario, Canada. 19" by 25". Design adapted by Gail Mueller from a photograph by Ann Hallett.

"A small group of us hook in the summer at Ann Hallett's farm in Coldwater, Ontario. I have always loved watching the sheep nibble their way around the barnyard and under the apple trees. When Ann taught 'Sheep' in 2002, I leapt at the chance to join in."

Mac Duff. Hooked by Angela Foote, Barrington, New Hampshire. 14" by 14". Designed by Jane McGown Flynn.

Summer on the Farm. Hooked by Marion Brown, Brunswick, Maine. 21" by 32". Designed by Sue Hamer.

Peace in Vermont. Hooked by Joan Hebert, Orleans, Vermont. 16" by 17". Designed by Nancy Urbanak of Beaver Brook Crafts.

Have You Any Wool? Hooked by Suzanne Kowalski, South Burlington, Vermont. 24" by 36". Designed by Woolley Fox LLC/Barb Carroll.
"The lamb's curly wool drew me to this whimsical rug. I found it at one of my first trips to The Dorr Mill Store in New Hampshire."

Cherries and Sheep. Hooked by Dick LaBarge, Victory Mills, New York. 50" by 29". Designed by Marion Ham – Quail Hill Designs.

Roger. Designed and hooked by Lisa Mulligan, Erie, Colorado. 24" by 33".
"This rug was designed for my love—he considers himself the black sheep of his family so that was the start. The heart is the love in his life, the star his success, and the three sheep are his daughters. The story of the rug tells him that, black sheep or no, he has a full rich life and is surrounded by those who love him."

Untitled. Designed and hooked by Susan O'Leary, Dorset, Vermont. 30" by 43".

"My first original design based on an adaptation of my first quilt. Thanks to the patience and generosity of Diane Kelly and Patty Yoder, who taught me how to dye the wool. Sheep is hooked with alpaca and angora that I did my best to card and pull through."

Keda, East Calais Sheep Goddess. Designed and hooked by Carla Straight, East Calais, Vermont. 9" by 6".

"Hungry to hook more after my first rug project, I sketched and hooked 'Keda' on Thanksgiving weekend 2004. This rug was purposefully left rough to emphasize the use of at-hand materials like the recycled burlap bag, yarns, and roving from 'the fiber stash.'"

Mizbah. Hooked by Ivi Nelson Collier, Nottingham, Maryland. 12" by 12". Designed by Tish Murphy.

"I found this pattern by Tish Murphy in a past issue of *Rug Hooking* magazine and knew it was the perfect Christmas gift for a dear wool-witch friend. I love how the pattern combines the shapes of the geometrics and the sheep. I love Mizbah's expression."

The Highland Clearances – Scotland. Designed and hooked by Roberta Smith, West Windsor, New Jersey. 29" by 54".

"In reading some Scottish history, I learned about the highland clearances when poor Highlanders were forced off the land. A loose translation of the Gaelic writing is, 'Woe is you O land because huge numbers of sheep are coming.' Cheviot sheep were imported to roam the land. Teacher: Jayne Hester."

Cows

Purple Cow. Hooked by Janet Myette, Glens Falls, New York. 26" by 32". Designed by George Kahnle for Hooked on the Creek.
"My love of cows prompted me to choose this wonderful design. A great pattern by George Kahnle! My first rug."

Family Cow. Designed and hooked by Rachel Jacobs, Montpelier, Vermont. 15" by 24".
"My great-granddaughter, Sage, wanted me to hook a black and white cow to represent her heritage."

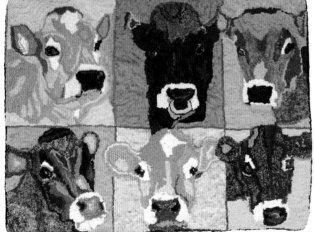

Cowmage to Patty Y. Designed and hooked by Carlie Dandridge, Kezar Falls, Maine. 25" by 32".
"Design inspired by a neighboring Guernsey farm and by Patty Yoder."

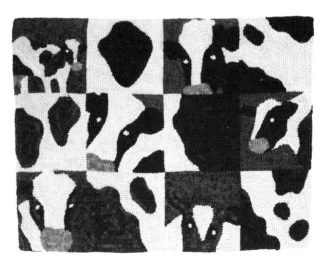

Cow Quilt. Hooked by Nola A. Heidbreder, Saint Louis, Missouri. 22" by 30". Designed by Cactus Needle.

Wool Bull. Designed and hooked by Diane Gage, Akron, Pennsylvania. 20" by 36". "Designed in the tradition of immortalizing a favorite farm animal. I used an antique weathervane for my model."

Happiness. Hooked by Nancy Spier, Jericho, Vermont. 15" diameter. Designed by Primitive Grace.

Elsie – Nicknamed Udder Chaos. Hooked by Terry Berntsen, Acworth, New Hampshire. 15" diameter. Designed by Cheri Raymond.
"We've had running black and white cow jokes with my friend Ron Lippard for years. The Christmas I hooked this rug, I promised no black and white cows. Voilà! A cow of another color."

Local Scenery. Designed and hooked by Lisa Mulligan, Erie, Colorado. 13" by 18".
"I frequently drive past this bull and company. They are typically gathered in a shady gully by the side of County Road #7 in Erie. I always slow or stop to say hi."

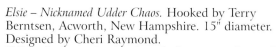

Wild Animals

Rufus. Designed and hooked by Beverly Conway, Beverly Conway Designs, Middlebury, Vermont. 27" by 46".
"Rufus was created in my imagination. I just love animals in rugs."

Lion. Hooked by Martha Beals, Sidney, Maine. 37" by 46".
Designed by Edyth C. O'Neill.

Sandy's Lion. Hooked by Sarah Guiliani, South Portland, Maine. 15" by 14". Designed by The House of Price, Inc.
"This was a pattern I taught at a workshop in Massachusetts. The idea was to teach fingering."

Zeus. Designed and hooked by Joyce Combs, Lambertville, New Jersey. 36" by 18".
"The inspiration for Zeus came from several photographs of walking tigers. I designed a simple background so Zeus would appear to be walking out of the forest towards the viewer of the rug. Zeus was started in a class with Elizabeth Black."

Jay's Tiger. Designed and hooked by M. Kay Weeks, Port Murray, New Jersey. 22" by 21".
"Designed from a multiple collection of tiger faces. I hooked this for a tiger show in Princeton, New Jersey. However, my husband fell in love with it and would not let the tiger leave our home. He now recognizes rug hooking talent. Hurrah!"

Elephants' Circus. Hooked by Sheila M. Breton, Surry, New Hampshire. 23" by 36". Designer unknown.
"This rug was started by my husband's grandmother, Helen McQueston, in 1951 (see date, lower left corner). I found it one-third done and I completed it in 2005. The edges were hooked through all the layers, covering the name and designer of the pattern."

Elabella – #5 in 'Girls Just Wanna Have Fun' Series. Hooked by Suzi Prather, Orlando, Florida. 29" by 39". Designed by DiFranza Designs.
"Elabella is a very rare elephant from Tuskany. She is an extremely plain elephant except for her eyelashes. (Some think her eyelashes are false, but no, they are her very own.) Elabella spends her days having fun by trying on different accessories. She says, 'It's all about accessories!' "

Regal Cats. Hooked by Theresa Strack, Bedford, New Hampshire. 31" by 38". Designed by Elizabeth Black. "I love to hook wild cats. These two 'regal' cheetahs were great fun to do."

Leah's Trip to South Africa. Designed and hooked by Layne G. Herschel, Chester, Vermont. 27" by 39". "My daughter, Leah, went to South Africa her sophomore year of college. The experience changed her view of the world."

Chapter 11

Abstracts

Tree Lines 3. Designed and hooked by Molly W. Dye, Jacksonville, Vermont. 8" by 12".
"I've attempted to depict nature in streams or ribbons of colors that flow and interact. Given the suggestions of objects, the mind will develop its own images and finish the statement."

Salisbury. Designed and hooked by Molly W. Dye, Jacksonville, Vermont. 38" by 32".
"Visiting Salisbury Plain, I was in awe of the turbulent skies full of energy and the relationship to planted fields of poppies, barley, purple flax, and other grains."

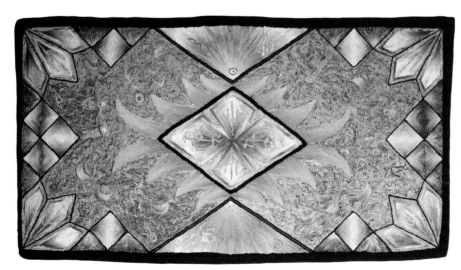

Arizona Journey. Designed and hooked by Angela Foote, Barrington, New Hampshire. 68" by 36".
"This rug was hooked to show the wonderful colors and shapes that we experienced on our trips throughout the southwest."

Red and Gold. Designed and hooked by Carolyn Buttolph of Red House Rugs, St. Johnsbury, Vermont. 12" by 12".

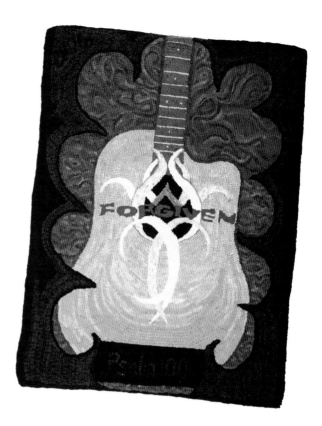

Keith's Forgiven. Designed and hooked by DonnaSue Shaw, Grand Isle, Vermont. 37" by 27".
"This rug was a challenge for me as I tend to go a little crazy with color and this palette was very limited. I did enjoy the process though. Special thanks to Life Epistles for allowing me to use their 'Forgiven Cross' in this rug designed for my son, Keith."

Tumbling Stars. Designed and hooked by Kathleen Harwood, Montrose, Pennsylvania. 29" by 40".
"A swirling evening sky, with stars like tumbling, blowing autumn leaves."

In Phyllis' Memory. Designed and hooked by Joan Wheeler, Newport, Vermont. 37" by 25".
"Phyllis started this before she died and her daughter gave it to me to complete. She started both ends but could not work on this rug due to her illness. I completed it using all my scrap pieces of wool."

Stained Glass Art Project. Designed and hooked by Alan S. Kidder, Rochester, Vermont. 36" by 29".
"This design is reminiscent of a math lesson I have used with these terms: horizontal, vertical, diagonal, and intersecting. Throw it all together with leftover scraps of wool—a stained glass effect."

What Should I Hook Today? Sampler. Designed and hooked by Joan Wheeler, Newport, Vermont. 29" by 18".
"Started with Diane Moore to practice our techniques. Then just became a fun thing to do each day. Anything that popped into my head went wherever—no planning!"

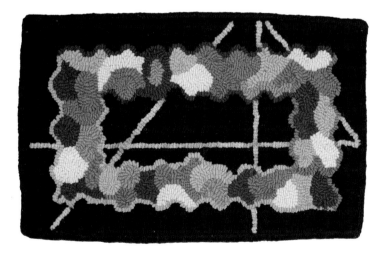

Paisley Challenge. Designed and hooked by Sara Burghoff, Underhill, Vermont. 14" by 14".
"I created this chair pad for the Cortina Inn paisley challenge. I used scraps of yarn and had a great time figuring out how to combine the colors. The paisleys are hooked traditionally, while the background is punch-hooked."

Curves and Lines. Designed and hooked by Marcy Harding, Jonesville, Vermont. 8" by 13".
"I created this mat using a Green Mountain Rug Hooking Guild kit from a class with Jen Lavoie. The colors were my attempt to improve with curves, the black background is for contrast, and the lines are to add interest."

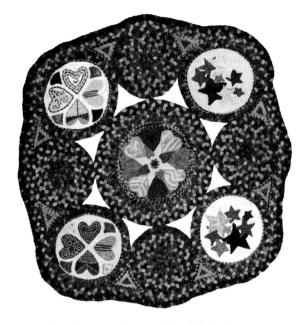

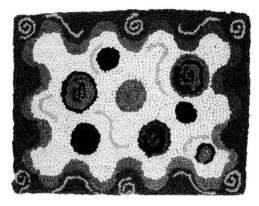

www.dot.edu. Designed and hooked by Clarissa Gage, Akron, Pennsylvania. 13" by 17".
"My mother taught me how to hook rugs this year during a school break. I created a simple design so that I would have time to complete it before heading back to college. This is my learning rug."

Lace. Designed and hooked by Kris McDermet, Dummerston, Vermont. 37" by 37".
"This rug started as a single chair pad. As hooked and braided circles were added, I began to appreciate the open fretwork appearance. The lace effect seemed to create a unique pattern between the floor and rug."

Lichen and Slate. Designed and hooked by Susan Feller, Augusta, West Virginia. 14" by 15".
"A sketch of Judy Quintman's flagstone patio in 2002 waited for me to learn punch needle. As the subject has multiple layers, I used wool fabric, attached with needle felting as flat planes and color plan—yarns, roving and beads, an argyle sweater was cut to size."

Crewel Tree. Hooked by Theresa Strack, Bedford, New Hampshire. 36" by 26".
"Design adapted by Theresa Strack from a bedcover pattern made available to the public in *Book of Patterns and Instructions for American Needlework*. The original homespun bedcover is from the Witte Memorial Museum, San Antonio, Texas. This is the corner motif from the bedcover."

Radio Rug. Designed and hooked by Carla Straight, East Calais, Vermont. 12" by 9".
"This rug was inspired by learning circuitry symbols for my amateur radio license in 2005. Unspun roving from my Jacob sheep forms the background for the symbols: Ground + Coil + Antenna = Radio."

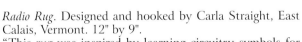

Chapter 12

Miniatures
Russian Punch Needle Embroidery

Portland Head Lighthouse, Maine. Designed and hooked by Ellen Hoffman, Cape Neddick, Maine. 3.5" by 5". "Portland Lighthouse evokes calm and connectedness to the ocean below. The crashing surf and wind all motivated me to create this piece. Sky is ever changing. Just a beautiful place to visit."

Nantucket Great Point Lighthouse. Designed and hooked by Ellen Hoffman, Cape Neddick, Maine. 5" by 3.5". "While living on Nantucket Island, we often took trips to Great Point for family picnics. It is one of the quietest places on the island. It holds fond memories of a place and time, back in the early 1980s, before it was discovered!"

Angel Baby – Fraktur Style. Hooked by Janet Myette, Glens Falls, New York. 4" by 5.5". Designed by George Kahnle for Hooked on the Creek.
 "Miniature punch needle version of my full size rug, 'Angel Queen – Fraktur Style.' " (See page 56.)

Weeping Willow. Hooked by LeeAnn Metropoulos, Lebanon, New Jersey. 5.5" by 7". Designed by Susan Feller, Ruckman Mill Farm.
"Punch needle embroidery of willow inspired by headstone designs c.1800 in East Randolph, Vermont cemetery."

153

Green Mountain Night. Designed and hooked by Linda Repasky, Amherst, Massachusetts. 2.25" by 3". "Miniature punch needle."

Us and Them. Designed and hooked by Kathleen Menzies, Greenfield Park, Quebec, Canada. 3" by 4". "This is a scene that is frequent around our house in late summer. While I appreciate the role played by wasps and bees in our ecosystem, I don't want them indoors."

1850 Floral. Designed and hooked by Janet Wagner, Rochester, New York. 3.75" by 2.5". "Miniature reproduction of an 1850 hooked rug; mounted on wool dyed with geraniums from designer's garden."

And the Cow Jumped Over the Moon. Hooked by Sarah Madison, Amherst, Massachusetts. 4.25" by 4.25". Design adapted from an illustration by David Carter Brown. "Inspired by an illustration by David Carter Brown. Adapted to serve as the birth record for Geneva Jean Bessette, January 27, 2005. Miniature Russian punch needle."

Starlit Meadow. Designed and hooked by Linda Repasky, Amherst, Massachusetts. 4" by 4.25".
"Miniature punch needle."

18th Century Carnation. Designed and hooked by Janet Wagner, Rochester, New York. 2.5" by 3".
"Adaptation of a 1761 embroidered pocketbook; mounted on hand-dyed wool."

Horatio. Designed and hooked by Linda Repasky, Amherst, Massachusetts. 2.25" by 3".
"Miniature punch needle."

St. George, Little Red Schoolhouse. Designed and hooked by Cyndi Melendy Labelle, Hinesburg, Vermont. 4" by 6".
"I did this miniature of the St. George Little Red Schoolhouse as a gift for a coworker. She is retiring from Champlain Valley Union High School this June. Her first teaching job was as the teacher at this schoolhouse in the 1960s. She was also the last teacher to teach at this school."

Antique Flower Basket. Designed and hooked by Janet Wagner, Rochester, New York. 1.75" by 3.25".
"Adaptation of an 1840 hooked rug."

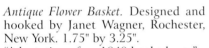

Prince Sasha. Designed and hooked by Janet Wagner, Rochester, New York. 3" by 4.25".
"Adaptation of 1895 hooked rug; mounted on wool natural-dyed with geraniums from designer's garden."

Little Sister's Bird. Designed and hooked by Janet Wagner, Rochester, New York. 2.5" by 3.75".
"Adaptation of an 1847 quilt piece named 'Little Sister's Quilt.' "

A Bouquet for Emeline. Designed and hooked by Linda Repasky, Amherst, Massachusetts. 2.25" by 3.5".
"Miniature punch needle."

Four Fraktur Flowers. Hooked by Lisa Mims, Flemington, New Jersey. 1.75" by 2.25" each. Designed by Susan Feller, Ruckman Mill Farm.
"Punch needle examples of Pennsylvania German designs illustrating frakturs (important documents)."

Rug Show Vendors

The following vendors exhibited at Hooked in the Mountains XI. They offered a diverse assortment of rug hooking supplies—everything one could possibly need to make a hooked rug: rug hooks, punch needles, patterns, rug backing, dyes, dyeing equipment, cloth cutting machines, specialty scissors, frames, finishing supplies, books, kits, rug yarn, an enormous assortment of beautiful wool fabric, and even hand-made baskets to put it all in. Their booths, decorated with their own exceptional rugs, were an exciting extension of the show itself.

Besides providing us with the finest quality goods and gift items, these vendors also offered reliable and expert advice. Many beginners have launched a first rug thanks to their help, while scores of seasoned rug hookers wait all year to shop in the round barn basement, stocking up for future projects. As we all know, you can never have too much wool. Thank you to all of these hard working individuals. The show wouldn't be the same without you.

American Country Rugs
Lucille Festa
4743 Route 315
Pawlet, VT 05761
(Studio located in East Rupert)
(802) 325-2543
E-mail: Lucillefesta@hotmail.com

Beaver Brook Crafts
Nancy Urbanak
4959 Squires Drive
Titusville, FL 32796
(321) 268-2193
E-mail: NancyUrbanak@yahoo.com

Beverly Conway Designs
Beverly Conway
1859 Munger Street
Middlebury, VT 05753
(802) 388-7742
E-mail: prism@together.net

The Dorr Mill Store
Terry Dorr
PO Box 88, 22 Hale Street
Guild, NH 03754
(603) 863-1197 or (800) 846-DORR
E-mail: dorrmillstore@nhvt.net
Website: DorrMillStore.com

Fluff & Peachy Bean Designs
Nancy D. Jewett
PO Box 30, 2126 US Route 7
Pittsford, VT 05763
(802) 483-2222
E-mail: njewett@aol.com

Green Mountain Hooked Rugs, Inc.
Stephanie Krauss
2838 County Road

Montpelier, VT 05602
(802) 223-1333
E-mail:
vtpansy@GreenMountainHookedRugs.com
Website: GreenMountainHookedRugs.com

Hooked Treasures
Cherylyn Brubaker
6 Iroquois Circle
Brunswick, ME 04011
(207) 729-1380
E-mail: tcbru@suscom-maine.net
Website: www.hookedtreasures.com

Kinderhook Bed & Breakfast
Jayne Hester
67 Broad Street
Kinderhook, NY 12106
(518) 758-1850
E-mail: Kinderhookb-b@Berk.com
Website: KinderhookBandB.com

Little Victories Rug Designs
Diane Phillips
19 Great Garland Rise
Fairport, NY 14450
(585) 223-0038
E-mail: rugsdp@rochester.rr.com

Liziana Creations
Diana and Liz O'Brien
595 Patten Hill Road, PO Box 310
Shelburne Falls, MA 01370
(413) 625-9403
E-mail, Diana: Diana@galaxy.net
E-mail, Liz: mikeandlizob@cox.net
Website: www.liziana.com

Primitive Spirit
Karen Kahle
PO Box 1363
Eugene, OR 97440
(541) 344-4316
E-mail: k_rathbun@hotmail.com
Website: PrimitiveSpiritRugs.com

R is 4 Rug
Jule Marie Smith
485 Sweetman Road
Ballston Spa, NY 12020
(518) 882-9215
E-mail: ris4rug@aol.com

Rae Harrell Rug Hooking Studio
Rae Harrell
154 Mallard Pond Road
Hinesburg, VT 05461
(802) 482-2076
E-mail: raeharrell@gmavt.net

Ruckman Mill Farm
Susan Feller
PO Box 409
Augusta, WV 26704
(304) 496-8073
E-mail: info@ruckmanmillfarm.com
Website: www.ruckmanmillfarm.com

Rugwool Studio
Judy Kohler
PO Box 398
Stanfordville, NY 12581
(845) 266-8093
E-mail: hooker@rugwool.com
Website: rugwoolstudio.com

The Singing Bird
Arlene Scanlon
18 South Hill Drive
Essex Junction, VT 05452
(802) 878-5917
E-mail: tsbarlene@yahoo.com

Susan Gingras Baskets
Susan Gingras
3004 Snake Mountain Road
Weybridge, VT 05753
(802) 545-2672
E-mail: suebea3004@yahoo.com

Townsend Industries, Inc.
Katie Lane
6650 NE 41st Street
Altoona, IA 50009
(515) 967-4261
E-mail: KatieL@T-51.com
Website: TownsendFabricCutter.com

Vermont Folk Rugs
Davey DeGraff
423 SW Shore Road
Hinesburg, VT 05461
(802) 482-2720
E-mail: daveyinvt@yahoo.com
Website: vermontfolkrugs.com

Violet Jane
Sara Burghoff
29 Maple Ridge Road
Underhill, VT 05489
(802) 899-3909
E-mail: sara@violetjane.com
Website: VioletJane.com

Wool Down Under
Karen Quigley
10 Sunset Drive
Vergennes, VT 05491
(802) 877-1561
E-mail: sunsetkq@yahoo.com

Suggested Reading

Compiled by Anne-Marie Littenberg

Books

Allard, Mary. *Rug Making: Techniques and Design*. Philadelphia, Pennsylvania: Chilton Book Company, 1963.

Aller, Doris. *Handmade Rugs*. Menlo Park, California: Lane Publishing Company, c. 1953.

Batchelder, Martha. *The Art of Hooked-Rug Making*. Peoria, Illinois: The Manual Arts Press, 1947.

Beatty, Alice, and Mary Sargent. *Basic Rug Hooking*. Harrisburg, Pennsylvania: Stackpole Books, 1990.

Beatty, Alice, and Mary Sargent. *The Hook Book*. Harrisburg, Pennsylvania: Stackpole Books, 1977.

Black, Elizabeth. *Hooked on the Wild Side*. Lemoyne, Pennsylvania: Rug Hooking Magazine, 2004.

Boswell, Thom, ed. *The Rug Hook Book: Techniques, Projects and Patterns for This Easy, Traditional Craft*. New York: Sterling Publishing Co., Inc., 1992.

Bramlett, Carol, and Leslie Hoy. *A Celebration of Hand-Hooked Rugs VIII*. Edited by Patrice A. Crowley. Harrisburg, Pennsylvania: Stackpole Books, 1998.

Brown, Barbara Evans. *Preserving the Past in Primitive Rugs*. Harrisburg, Pennsylvania: Stackpole Books, 2005.

Burton, Mary Sheppard. *A Passion for the Creative Life: Textiles to Lift the Spirit*. Edited by Mary Ellen Cooper. Germantown, Maryland: Sign of the Hook Books, 2002.

A Celebration of Hand-Hooked Rugs. Harrisburg, Pennsylvania: Stackpole Books, 1991.

Carroll, Barbara. *The Secrets of Primitive Hooked Rugs: Your Complete Guide to Hooking a Primitive Rug*. Harrisburg, Pennsylvania: Stackpole Publications, 2004.

Carroll, Barbara. *Woolley Fox American Folk Art Rug Hooking*. Urbandale, Iowa: Landauer Corporation, 2005.

Cooper, Mary Ellen, ed. *A Celebration of Hand-Hooked Rugs II*. Harrisburg, Pennsylvania: Stackpole Books, 1992.

Cooper, Mary Ellen, ed. *A Celebration of Hand-Hooked Rugs III*. Harrisburg, Pennsylvania: Stackpole Books, 1993.

Cox, Verna. *Rug Hooking and Braiding Made Easy*. Atlanta, Georgia: Cox Enterprises, 2003.

Crouse, Gloria E. *Hooking Rugs: New Materials, New Techniques* (and companion video). Newtown, Connecticut: The Taunton Press, 1990.

Cross, Pat. *Purely Primitive: Hooked Rugs from Wool, Yarn, and Homespun Scraps*. Woodinville, Washington: Martingale and Company, 2003.

Cross, Pat. *Simply Primitive: Rug Hooking, Punchneedle, and Needle Felting*. Woodinville, Washington: Martingale and Company, 2006.

Crowley, Patrice A., ed. *A Celebration of Hand-Hooked Rugs V*. Harrisburg, Pennsylvania: Stackpole Books, 1995.

Crowley, Patrice A., ed. *A Celebration of Hand-Hooked Rugs VI*. Harrisburg, Pennsylvania: Stackpole Books, 1996.

Crowley, Patrice A., ed. *A Celebration of Hand-Hooked Rugs VII*. Harrisburg, Pennsylvania: Stackpole Books, 1997.

Crowley, Patrice A., ed. *A Rug Hooker's Garden*. Harrisburg, Pennsylvania: Rug Hooking Magazine, 2000.

Darr, Tara. *Wool Rug Hooking*. Iola, Wisconsin: Krause Publications, 2005.

Davies, Ann. *Rag Rugs: How to Use Ancient and Modern Rug-Making Techniques to Create Rugs, Wallhangings, Even Jewelry – 12 Projects*. New York: Henry Holt and Company, Inc., 1992.

Davis, Mildred J. *The Art of Crewel Embroidery*. New York: Crown Publishing, 1962.

Davis, Mildred J. *Early American Embroidery Designs*. New York: Crown Publishing, 1969.

Davis, Mildred J., ed. *Embroidery Designs, 1780-1820; From the manuscript collection, The Textile Resource and Research Center, the Valentine Museum, Richmond, Virginia*. New York, Crown Publishing, 1971.

Eber, Dorothy H. *Catherine Poirier's Going Home Song*. Halifax, Nova Scotia: Nimbus Publishing, 1994.

Farr, Christopher, Mathew Bourne, and Fiona Leslie. *Contemporary Rugs*. London: Merrell Publishers Limited, 2002.

Felcher, Cecelia. *The Complete Book of Rug Making: Folk Methods and Ethnic Designs*. New York: Hawthorne Books, 1975.

Field, Jeanne. *Shading Flowers: The Complete Guide for Rug Hookers*. Harrisburg, Pennsylvania: Stackpole Books, 1991.

Fitzpatrick, Deanne. *Hook Me A Story: The History and Method of Rug Hooking in Atlantic Canada*. Halifax, Nova Scotia: Nimbus Publishing, Ltd., 1999.

Halliwell, Jane E. *The Pictorial Rug: Everything You Need to Know to Hook a Realistic, Impressionistic, or Primitive Picture With Wool*. Rug Hooking Magazine's Framework Series 2000, Edition V. Lemoyne, Pennsylvania: M. David Detweiler, 2000.

Henry Ford Museum & Greenfield Village. *Edward Sands Frost's Hooked Rug Patterns*. Dearborn, Michigan: Edison Institute, 1970.

Hoy, Leslie, and Sarah Wilt. *A Celebration of Hand-Hooked Rugs IX*. Edited by Patrice A. Crowley. Harrisburg, Pennsylvania: Stackpole Books, 1999.

Hoy, Leslie. *A Celebration of Hand-Hooked Rugs X*. Edited by Patrice A. Crowley. Harrisburg, Pennsylvania: Stackpole Books, 2000.

Hoy, Leslie. *A Celebration of Hand-Hooked Rugs XI*. Edited by Patrice A. Crowley. Lemoyne, Pennsylvania: Rug Hooking Magazine, 2001.

Hoy, Leslie. *A Celebration of Hand-Hooked Rugs XII*. Edited by Wyatt R. Myers. Lemoyne, Pennsylvania: Rug Hooking Magazine, 2002.

Johnson, Barbara. *American Classics: Hooked Rugs from the Barbara Johnson Collection*. Jenkintown, Pennsylvania. Squibb Corp., 1988.

Kennedy, MacDonald, ed. *A Celebration of Hand-Hooked Rugs IV*. Harrisburg, Pennsylvania: Stackpole Books, 1994.

Kent, William W. *The Hooked Rug*. New York: Tudor Publishing Company, 1930.

Kent, William W. *Hooked Rug Design*. Springfield, Massachusetts: The Pond-Ekberg Company, 1949.

Kent, William W. *Rare Hooked Rugs and Other: Both Antique & Modern*. Springfield, Massachusetts: The Pond-Ekberg Company, 1941.

Ketchum, William C., Jr. *Hooked Rugs: A Historical and Collectors Guide: How to Make Your Own*. New York: Harcourt, Brace, Jovanovich, 1976.

King, Mrs. Harry. *How To Hook Rugs*. Little Rock, Arkansas: D. P. and L. Company, 1948.

Kopp, Joel, and Kate Kopp. *American Hooked and Sewn Rugs: Folk Art Underfoot*. New York: E. P. Dutton, Inc., 1985.

Lais, Emma Lou, and Barbara Carroll. *Antique Colours for Primitive Rugs: Formulas Using Cushing Acid Dyes*. Kennebunkport, Maine: W. Cushing & Company, 1996.

Lais, Emma Lou, and Barbara Carroll. *American Primitive Hooked Rugs: Primer for Recreating Antique Rugs*. Kennebunkport, Maine: Wildwood Press, 1999.

Lawless, Dorothy. *Rug Hooking and Braiding For Pleasure and Profit*. New York: Thomas Y. Crowell, 1962.

Lincoln, Maryanne. *Recipes From the Dye Kitchen*. Harrisburg, Pennsylvania: Rug Hooking Magazine, 1999.

Lincoln, Maryanne. *Maryanne Lincoln's Comprehensive Dyeing Guide*. Lemoyne, Pennsylvania: Rug Hooking Magazine, 2005.

Linsley, Leslie. *Hooked Rugs: An American Folk Art*. New York: Clarkson N. Potter, Inc., 1992.

Logsdon, Roslyn. *People and Places: Roslyn Logsdon's Imagery In Fiber*. Rug Hooking Magazine's 1998 Framework Series

Edition. Harrisburg, Pennsylvania: David Detweiler, 1998.

Lovelady, Donna. *Rug Hooking For the First Time*. New York: Sterling Chapelle, 2005.

Mather, Anne D. *Creative Rug Hooking*. New York: Sterling Publishing Company, 2000.

McGown, Pearl K. *Color in Hooked Rugs*. West Boylston, Massachusetts: Pearl K. McGown, 1954.

McGown, Pearl K. *The Lore and Lure of Hooked Rugs*. West Boylston, Massachusetts: Pearl K. McGown, 1966.

McGown, Pearl K. *Persian Patterns*. West Boylston, Massachusetts: Pearl K. McGown, 1958.

McGown, Pearl K. *You...Can Hook Rugs*. West Boylston, Massachusetts: Pearl K. McGown, 1951.

Minick, Polly and Laurie Simpson. *Everyday Folk Art: Hooked Rugs and Quilts to Make*. Woodinville, Washington: Martingale and Company, 2005.

Minick, Polly and Laurie Simpson. *Folk Art Friends: Hooked Rugs and Coordinating Quilts*. Woodinville, Washington: Martingale and Company, 2003.

Montell, Joseph. *The Art of Speed Tufting*. Santa Ana, California: RC Rug Crafters, 1976.

Moshimer, Joan. *The Complete Rug Hooker: A Guide to the Craft*. Boston, Massachusetts: New York Graphic Society, 1975.

Moshimer, Joan. *Hooked on Cats: Complete Patterns and Instructions for Rug Hookers*. Harrisburg, Pennsylvania: Stackpole Books, 1991.

Myer, Wyatt, ed., *Basic Rug Hooking*. Lemoyne, Pennsylvania: Rug Hooking Magazine, 2002.

Myers, Lori. *A Celebration of Hand-Hooked Rugs XIII: The Finest of Fiber Art*. Edited by Wyatt R. Myers. Lemoyne, Pennsylvania: Rug Hooking Magazine, 2003.

Olson, Jane. *The Rug Hooker's Bible: The Best from 20 Years of Jane Olson's Rugger's Roundtable*. Edited by Gene Shepherd. Harrisburg, Pennsylvania: Stackpole Publications 2006.

Oxford, Amy. *Hooked Rugs Today*. Atglen, Pennsylvania: Schiffer Publishing Ltd., 2004.

Oxford, Amy. *Punch Needle Rug Hooking: Techniques and Designs*. Atglen, Pennsylvania: Schiffer Publishing Ltd., 2003.

Parker, Xenia L. *Hooked Rugs & Ryas: Designing Patterns and Applying Techniques*. Chicago, Illinois: Henry Regency Company, 1973.

Peladeau, Mildred C. *Art Underfoot: The Story of the Waldoboro Hooked Rugs*. Lowell, Massachusetts: American Textile History Museum, 1999.

Peverill, Sue. *Make Your Own Rugs: A Guide to Design and Technique*. London: Hamlyn Publishing Group, Ltd., 1989.

Phillips, Anna M. *Hooked Rugs and How to Make Them*. New York: Macmillan, 1925.

Ries, Estelle H. *American Rugs*. Cleveland, Ohio: The World Publishing Company, 1950.

Rex, Stella H. *Choice Hooked Rugs*. New York: Prentice-Hall, 1953.

Rex, Stella H. *Practical Hooked Rugs*. Ashville, Maine: Cobblesmith, 1975.

Rug Hooking Magazine – the entire *Framework and Celebrations* series.

A Rug Hooking Book of Days Featuring the Fiber Art of Polly Minick. Harrisburg, Pennsylvania: Stackpole Books, 1998.

Rug Hooker's Garden: 10 Experts Teach You How to Hook a Veritable Bouquet of Blossoms. Harrisburg, Pennsylvania, Stackpole Books, 2005.

Siano, Margaret and Susan Huxley. *The Secrets of Finishing Hooked Rugs*. Lemoyne, Pennsylvania: Rug Hooking Magazine, 2003.

Stratton, Charlotte K. *Rug Hooking Made Easy*. New York: Harper and Brothers Publishers, 1955.

Taylor, Mary P. *How To Make Hooked Rugs*. Philadelphia: David McKay Company, c. 1930.

Tennant, Emma. *Rag Rugs of England and America*. London: Walker Books, 1992.

Turbayne, Jessie A. *The Big Book of Hooked Rugs: 1950s-1980s*. Atglen, Pennsylvania: Schiffer Publishing Ltd., 2004.

Turbayne, Jessie A. *Hooked Rugs: History and The Continuing Tradition*. West Chester, Pennsylvania: Schiffer Publishing Ltd., 1991.

Turbayne, Jessie A. *Hooked Rug Treasury*. Atglen, Pennsylvania: Schiffer Publishing Ltd., 1997.

Turbayne, Jessie A. *The Hooker's Art*. Atglen, Pennsylvania: Schiffer Publishing Ltd., 1993.

Turbayne, Jessie A. *The Complete Guide to Collecting Hooked Rugs: Unrolling the Secrets*. Atglen, Pennsylvania: Schiffer Publishing Ltd., 2004.

Underhill, Vera B., and Arthur J. Burks. *Creating Hooked Rugs*. New York: Coward-McCann, 1951.

Vail, Juju. *Rag Rugs: Techniques in Contemporary Craft Projects*. Edison, New Jersey: Chartwell Books, 1997.

Von Rosenstiel, Helene. *American Rugs and Carpets From the Seventeenth Century to Modern Times*. New York: Morrow, c. 1978.

Walch, Margaret, and Augustine Hope. *Living Colors: The Definitive Guide to Color Palettes Through the Ages*. San Francisco: Chronicle Books, 1995.

Waugh, Elizabeth. *Collecting Hooked Rugs*. New York, London: The Century Company, 1927.

Wilcox, Bettina. *Hooked Rugs for Fun and Profit, With Original Hooked Rugs, Designs and Patterns From Famous Museum Collections*. New York: Homecrafts, c. 1949.

Wiseman, Ann. *Hand Hooked Rugs and Rag Tapestries*. New York: Van Nostrand Reinhold Company, Inc., 1969.

Yoder, Patty. *The Alphabet of Sheep*. Raleigh, North Carolina: Ivy House Publishing Group, 2003.

Yoder, Patty, ed. *Green Mountain Rug Hooking Guild Dye Book*. Tinmouth, Vermont: Green Mountain Rug Hooking Guild, 2003.

Young, Arthur. *America Gets Hooked: History of a Folk Art*. Lewiston, Maine: Booksplus, 1994.

Zarbok, Barbara J. *The Complete Book of Rug Hooking*. Princeton, New Jersey: D. Van Nostrand Company, Inc., 1961.

Periodicals

Fiberarts, 67 Broadway, Asheville, North Carolina 28801

Rug Hooking Magazine, 1300 Market St., Suite 202, Lemoyne, Pennsylvania 17043-1420

Wool Street Journal, 312 Custer Ave., Colorado Springs, Colorado 80903

Membership Information

The Green Mountain Rug Hooking Guild began in 1981 when a group of dedicated rug hookers from Vermont decided to form a guild. Their purpose was to make it possible to meet twice a year, to share their joy of rug hooking, and to learn from each other and outside speakers.

As a new guild member, you will receive a packet of information that includes a full membership list, by-laws, a teacher and supplier list, and the most recent issue of our quarterly newsletter. We are able to provide you with a listing of members in your immediate area, and can refer you to representatives and teachers. Our newsletter keeps everyone current because many are unable to attend the fall and spring meetings. In addition to these benefits, members get to exhibit their rugs at our annual show. They can also participate in our education programs, getting materials and tools for their volunteer teaching efforts.

To join the guild, please visit our web site:

www.greenmountainrughookingguild.org